D1328527

AN EDWARDIAN YOUTH

AN EDWARDIAN
YOUTH

BY

L. E. JONES

LONDON

MACMILLAN & CO LTD

NEW YORK · ST MARTIN'S PRESS

1956

MACMILLAN AND COMPANY LIMITED
London Bombay Calcutta Madras Melbourne

THE MACMILLAN COMPANY OF CANADA LIMITED
Toronto

ST MARTIN'S PRESS INC
New York

PRINTED IN GREAT BRITAIN

I

My grandfather, father and uncle had inhabited, in turn, the same set of rooms in Neville's Court at Trinity, Cambridge, and when Mr. St. John Parry, the Dean, limped up the stairs to show me these family rooms, with a promise that I, too, should occupy them in due course, it never crossed his mind or mine that two years later I should be going up to Balliol instead. Looking out from these rooms at the splendour of Wren's Library, I did not then reflect sadly, as I should today, how little my grandfather or father had profited from the possession of a room with that view. One would have expected that a young man, daily confronted with beauty in so solid and monumental a shape, would have received the imprint of some moral principles strong enough to preserve him for life from architectural wrong-doing. In fact, it was not so. My grandfather, who could afford it, sinned repeatedly, and my father, too poor for sins of commission, could approve or tolerate every kind of naughtiness in buildings. It is barely possible that the pair of them were shocked into cynicism by Wren's own grievous lapse in supporting the bold arches of the lower windows with uprights (a structural insult no true arch can bear) ; but it is unlikely, for an eye that could detect the blemish would also have seen why it must be forgiven.

I

How I came, as an Eton boy, to spend a couple of nights in the Dean's guest-chamber I do not remember. It may have been 'long leave', for it was term-time at Cambridge, and I dined with the Dons at the High Table, and drank port with them in the Senior Common Room, and became very talkative indeed. I still recollect my astonishment at learning that a very young Don, with a fresh complexion and twinkling eyes, was a 'Philosopher'; how, I asked Mr. Parry in a whisper, could one so young have become so wise? Mr. Parry gave me away, and they filled up my glass and entertained themselves with my cheek and naïveté, making me guess, from each man's face, what subject he professed or taught. They were kindly and merry and I saw nothing to confirm an experience told to me years later by A. L. Smith, the Master of Balliol. As a guest of honour at this same High Table he once sat at the Master's right hand, and so engaging was the Master's conversation that not until dinner was all but over did 'A. L.' remember that he had spoken no word to the Fellow of Trinity sitting on his other side. So he turned to him with some conventional, polite words, whereupon his neighbour turned scarlet, choked, dropped his fork, knocked over his wine-glass, and was thrown into a state of complete disorder. The Master of Trinity turned again to 'A. L.' 'I forgot to warn you,' he said, 'we never speak to the Mathematicians.'

The Dean could not be expected to give his whole attention to a schoolboy, and I was handed over to spend an evening in the rooms of an undergraduate whose name I have forgotten, and to find myself on a staircase adjoining the majestic Gateway, under which, in my father's day, a freshman once happened to be

sheltering from a sudden thunderstorm in company
with Dr. Hepworth Thompson, the Master. Thinking,
erroneously, that to be marooned in common justifies,
and even demands, some flicker of mutual awareness
between fellow-creatures, the shy young man ventured
upon a remark.

'A heavy storm, Master,' he said.

'All communications to the Master of the College
must be made through the Tutor,' was Dr. Thompson's
reply.

My host's rooms looked across the Great Court to
the Master's lodgings, and he described to me how,
when the last lights had been extinguished in the
Master's rooms, he would signal across the Court in
Morse Code, by switching on and off the newly in-
stalled electric light. Soon, answering signals would be
flashed from the Master's lodgings, but not by the
Master ; they would come from the bedroom of
Queenie, the Master's pretty daughter. I felt exhilarated
at being made privy to such goings-on, and admired his
bold ways with the daring and responsive Queenie.

But a deeper impression was made upon me by
another guest in these rooms — an undergraduate who
struck me as unbelievably mature, almost world-weary.
His long, ugly, bony face was pock-marked like a
photograph of the moon, but his eyes held me : sombre,
patient, unhappy eyes of extraordinary intelligence.
He held the talk ; he was sophisticated and mocking,
and more amusing, I thought, than anyone I had ever
met. After my return to Eton, I was astonished and
flattered to get a letter from this seasoned and salty
adult inviting me to spend a week of my summer
holidays bird-watching at his home. I wrote to my

parents for permission, and they in turn consulted Mr.
Parry. He replied that he could not take the responsibility of approving Edwin Montagu as a host to a
seventeen-year-old Eton boy. So I missed the chance
of making friends with an older man whose subtle and
sensitive mind would, I cannot but think, have brought
me nothing but good. I was indignant, but can hardly,
in retrospect, blame my parents. But would a Dean
of Trinity today consider a reference to 'very rich
Jews' relevant to the question asked of him ? I hope
not.

John Christie spat over the banisters, shouting : 'We
always spit the parting-guest' as I went downstairs, and
I had no presentiments of Glyndebourne ; but I
wandered back to Mr. Parry's rooms spellbound by my
glimpse of undergraduate life, and with the reassurance
that when I should come to die from the dear, familiar
world of Eton it would be but a passing to a Better
Place. And indeed, Oxonian to the marrow as I now
am, it is to Cambridge that I owe my first intoxicating
taste of the peculiar exhilaration, the almost continuous
inward excitement, that I was to experience during my
four years at Balliol. Should I have felt it at a modern,
'red-brick' University ? I am sure that I should not ;
and if so, the experience is not to be imputed to any
atmosphere of learning, to the Dons, to the communal
life, to the unaccustomed freedoms, or to the grateful
exchanges of friendship. All these can no doubt be
enjoyed at Reading. So the source of this strange per-
sistent sense of heightened and privileged living must,
it seems, be looked for in the material, and not in the
spiritual, qualities of Oxford and Cambridge ; in the
old stones themselves ; in so much beauty in so small

a space. The Colleges and University Buildings which crowd together, massive or graceful, soaring in towers and pinnacles or settling themselves in classic attitudes upon lawns broad enough to take their longest shadows, dispense their influences regardless of the Dons and Deans. The little streets that divide them, the Turl or Holywell or Merton Lane, no less than the High or the Broad or King's Parade which assemble and display them, reinforce their powers, and you discover in those narrow thoroughfares a backway to intimacy with the numinous and ancient walls that enclose them. 'Numinous'? When I have just said 'material'? Well, that, I suppose, is the mystery of Oxford, and of Cambridge too.

So I went back to Eton knowing, as I have said, that I had proofs of an 'Hereafter'. My change of allegiance was gradual. It may have begun with outings to Oxford with Mr. Rayner-Wood in Eights Week. I wished he could have omitted, 'It is very good of me to propose this, Jones', but it was indeed kind of him, and although his brisk and sergeant-major-like airs and breezy exchanges with Mike Furse on the towpath came a little between me and my earlier taste of romance at Cambridge, luncheon in Mr. Raper's rooms in Trinity did much to restore so slight a loss of enchantment. For Mr. Raper, the Bursar of Trinity, was a legendary figure, both as wit and savourer of good things, and in his slight, spare presence, with scanty beard and faintly mocking smile, Mr. Rayner-Wood's breeziness died away. And it was to me that Mr. Raper addressed himself, humorously, silkily, making more of the boy than of the Master. 'Why not Trinity, Oxford?' he asked, and, flushed with Mr. Raper's

claret and looking from his tall windows at the tender
greens of May, I came near to asking myself 'Why
not ?'

It was fortunate for me, perhaps, that nobody drew
my attention to the striped campanile of Balliol Chapel
looking over the Trinity wall, or to the Scottish-
baronial building with which Balliol abases the Broad.
Like that of an ugly woman with many lovers, Balliol's
uncomeliness only serves to underline the greatness and
ardour of her soul ; but I might, even in those days,
have been scared away by her looks, had I seen her in
the stone before hearing her talked about. As it turned
out, I did not see her ; and her lovers at Eton, Mr.
C. H. K. Marten and Tuppy Headlam, were long past
the stage of minding, or being even conscious of, the
physical failings of that fascinating *belle-laide*. For
Henry Marten had no doubts about the proper destina-
tion for his History specialists, as a few of us were
called. 'Embusqués' from the rigours of the Classics,
and from the absurdity of sharing lessons with the
Daniel Macmillans and the Gordon Selwyns, we had
our self-respect restored to us in Marten's cosy sitting-
room in Weston's Yard. It was Marten who explained
to me that Cambridge was all very well, but that
Balliol happened to be situated at Oxford, and that if
one wished to savour one's living as well as to earn it,
Balliol had secrets to impart which other colleges had
not. This vital information I passed on to my father
who, as credulous as he was open-minded, cheerfully
swallowed it ; and after Chris Goschen, a present
Balliol undergraduate, had corroborated Marten, and
Mr. F. F. Urquhart, the Junior Dean, had turned up at
Paris Plage, in those days a remote, unfrequented beach

where only an Urquhart could conceivably have been encountered, the thing was settled.

Mr. Raper's luncheon-table on a bright May day was one thing ; dark, low-ceilinged diggings in a cul-de-sac off Holywell in a December fog were quite another ; but the spell worked again, even more potently, when I went up to sit for the Balliol Scholarship examinations. In these I was twice lucky ; once, because I was asked to write a character of Robespierre and, thanks to Marten's prescience, was able to do so without quoting 'sea-green incorruptible' ; and a second time, because H. W. C. Davis, the celebrated 'Fluffy', did not share his colleagues' views that the papers of an Eton oarsman of good character were not worth reading. For the Dons had decided that I would 'do' on a letter from Marten, and my papers were thrown, unread, into the waste-paper basket. 'Fluffy', who had small interest in athletics, retrieved them, expecting to find evidence, with which to confound his fellow-Dons, that I was not up to Balliol standards. Whether he fished out the Character of Robespierre first of all I cannot say, but it ended with a Brackenbury Exhibition for me worth sixty pounds a year, to everybody's surprise. All this 'Fluffy' told me some years later, when he had spurred and whipped and driven me, with an uncanny insight into the minds of Examiners, to a First Class in Modern History. But at the time I was not even aware of his existence, and it was A. L. Smith who interviewed us and left me, for one, convinced that at Balliol, should I gain admittance, I might discover a way of life as well as a place of learning. For this square, sun-burnt, whiskered man, with broad forehead and furrowed cheeks, wearing

loose brown clothes and a flannel shirt, was everything
that I had not looked for in a Don. Needing no protective ceremony, he talked to us without condescension,
but with authority in his eye and in the certainty of his
warm, male voice. If this was a Don, one thought,
what could 'donnish' mean ? We returned to Eton
with the suspicion that 'A. L.' might expect us to be
less pupils than men.

This visit to Oxford was fifty years ago, when social
were as clearly defined as geological strata, and it never
occurred to us not to be amused at John Palmer, who
came up for examination in knickerbockers and strapped
shoes, and with a small school cap on the back of his
head. There was another candidate from Scotland who
wore a dicky but no shirt, and as he leant over his
papers across the long table, I caught disconcerting
glimpses of a naked chest. John Palmer won the
Brackenbury Scholarship and became a well-known
dramatic critic, but I do not remember seeing the shirt-
less one again. Neither our Christianity nor any native
generosity in us deterred us from making fun among
ourselves of these fellow-creatures, but I think we were
privately moved, however slightly, by the contrast
between their lot and our own. They were pushing
hard to open a door which for us had been always ajar.

If birds of a feather flock together, with young
Englishmen it is largely a question of pronunciation.
We could respect any one of our fellow-undergraduates ;
but a man going up to Oxford does not want respect,
he wants social equality, and for that — I tell of the
past — he must speak the Queen's English with a
specific accent and intonation. Or rather, he must *not*
speak it in certain ways ; for while a Scottish accent

can be so easy upon the ear that the speaker actually endears himself for that alone, and Yorkshire vowels can charm, a Cockney voice, in any of its variations, is a sad bar to social acceptance. (Even today I find that I am not alone in having difficulty in believing that the distinguished philosophers and scientists who talk to us in Cockney tones on the Third Programme can truly be men of learning, so indestructible is prejudice.)

In flocking with those of our own manner of speech I do not think we were consciously more snobbish than the rooks or the lapwings, but by acting upon the level of these instinctive creatures I have little doubt that we missed a good deal. A. L. Smith would have been sure of it, and A. D. Lindsay surer still, and there must be many men living who owe to these two Masters of Balliol their first break-through of the social 'sound-barrier'. Things are different today ; and it may well be that in another generation the mark of good breeding in a society of B.B.C.-standardised speech will be to cherish and conserve the various dialects of this ancient realm. May there then be a Master of Balliol to encourage the shy freshman who arrives speaking like an English gentleman of today not to be too much abashed by the members of the Annandale Society talking like Mr. J. B. Priestley !

It was something of a surprise, on first arriving, a little nervously, at the Main entrance of Balliol, to hear the head-porter, Hancock, greet me by name. I had been in and out of the College several times a day, with about fifty others, nine months earlier, but that was enough for Hancock. This smiling, square-built, blue-eyed man, with the ruddy countryman's look of a gamekeeper, never forgot a name or a face ; he never

forgot perfect manners; he never forgot his duty.
With all his natural kindliness for us all, it was no good
hoping that a breach of a College rule, however slight
or venial, would fail to be reported. He was incorruptible even by his own soft heart. Hancock knew
our characters as well as our names and gave us, not only
his experienced help in a hundred small problems, but
his friendship. Serviceable and alert, he stood for hours
behind the counter in his cubby-hole at the side of the
porch, never tired and never ruffled. All his loyalty
was to the Master and Fellows, all his interest in our
doings. Whatever our cliques and divisions among
ourselves, whatever the varying degrees of warmth felt
for this or that one of the Dons, Balliol men were
united, generation after generation, in their opinion of
Hancock. They all loved him. And he bequeathed to
the College a tradition which survived him, for in Cyril
King he had a successor worthy of himself.

I do not know how College rooms are allotted to
freshmen, but I was fortunate, for I found myself in a
ground-floor set on the celebrated — or should it be
notorious? — Number XIV staircase, with Gladstone's
profile, incised by Edmond Warre, and 'LUMPS — no
religious bias' indelibly engraved upon the stones beside
my window. Our rooms were not over-furnished;
there was a heavy square table in the middle of the
room, a bookcase, a few hard chairs and one arm-chair.
But this arm-chair was no ordinary one; it had a
wooden shelf for supporting a glass, attached to the
left-hand, and a solid oak book-rest revolving in a
socket screwed into the right-hand, arm. It was not
merely comfortable; it was an invitation to reading.
There was a kettle on the hob for heating bath-water,

little used by me, since I was still benighted enough to
splash in the shallow, icy, inch-deep saucer-bath which
leaned, like a cart-wheel, against the drab bedroom wall.
But breakfast was carried in hot from the kitchen by
Turner, my ancient scout, and laid on the fireplace,
the plate being protected by a circular pewter cover.
(Trollies loaded with these giant metal pill-boxes did
the round of the staircases every morning except
Sunday, when we breakfasted together in College Hall.)
Turner was a faithful and dependable, but not a com-
forting, servant. He was a grumbler. 'If that there
'onerble 'Erbert thinks 'e can turn this 'ere staircase into
'is play-'ole, 'e'll find 'e's mistook', was one of Turner's
overheard remarks, made in a moment of disgruntle-
ment. But it was probably 'Batey', the under-porter,
who took up my bags in the porch and escorted me for
the first time to these rooms where I was to spend three
years. 'Batey's' grammar was original : 'Yes, 'e 'ad
to went' was how he described the dismissal of a fellow-
scout, but he was a general favourite, for his idiom, his
good humour, and for something absurd and endearing
about his un-menial moustache.

I arrived with a bunch of Eton friends, and had to
conceal, except from Douglas Radcliffe who shared it,
my inner excitement at being a Balliol man, at being
an Oxonian. With Percy Perryman, a sturdy humorist
who steadfastly played poker to distract himself from
heavy private burdens, I discussed tobacco and pipes
and whisky ; he knew all that should be known about
these insignia of manhood. Eric Romilly was our tame
cynic, our pocket Voltaire ; he had picked up irreverent
tales about 'Paravi', his classical tutor, even before the
rest of us had conceived that the Dons might have

private lives at all. But Douglas and I knew that all
this amusing business of being men, of smoking pipes
and drinking whisky and talking bold little blasphemies
about God and the Dons, was surface-stuff. Not that
we mentioned it to one another ; it would have made
us shamefaced, and in any case there was no need for
speech — we had only to walk out into the Quad at
night, when even Hall loomed up majestically, or down
the Turl or Holywell, where the October fog softened
the lamplight and increased the mystery of those narrow
streets, to recover our sense of romance. For 'romance',
I suppose, is the only word for an emotional response to
a place or a person which causes continuous excitement
in those from whom it is evoked. It is not just beauty
that provokes the stir, for it can be strongest at night
or, as I have just said, in a fog ; nor just mystery, for
the closest acquaintance, in the clearest light of summer,
with Oxford's grey stones did not allay it. There
must be a sense, as well, of belonging to something
old, and honourable, and beneficent ; a sense of being
possessed as well as of possessing. It is agreeable to be
so stirred, and if there are obligations to be accepted,
they do not lull the excitement.

I had so much enjoyed grandeur during my last year
at Eton that I was quite unprepared, on arriving at
Oxford, for the surge of pleasure I felt at being a
nobody again. It was like the moment for taking off
one's stick-up collar and tail-coat after a long sultry
July day at the Eton and Harrow match. Irresponsi-
bility is a great refreshment, and on leaving boyhood
for good I felt five years younger. I was in charge of
nothing, had no dignity to maintain, and was out to
enjoy myself. But this 'lower-boy' mood had its pit-

falls. It was the custom for all the members of Number XIV staircase to lunch together in my sitting-room on cold meat and bread-and-jam, and in no time I had endangered my social position by removing Archie Gordon's cap from his head while he sat at table. Archie was almost inarticulate with rage and astonishment; 'the bloody freshman' was all he could stammer; but Alec Cadogan, even then competent to handle an awkward incident with the cool and equable common sense which later distinguished him at Lake Success, came to my rescue. He ruled that a mere freshman, in his own rooms and at his own table, might expect even second-year men to eat bareheaded, and that Archie should not have refused, as he did, to remove his cloth cap before meat. Molotov may, on occasions, have contested a ruling by Alec Cadogan; but we others, and Archie among us, never did. So I was forgiven, with that endearing grin which was to illumine so many reconciliations between Archie's warm heart and native turbulence. But why recollect a thing so much less than a petty skirmish? I record it, I think, because I was not always to escape so easily from the consequences of my naïve assumption that seniority has no relevance in matters of conduct or opinion. I was slowly to learn, by the hard way, that to a high degree in most relationships, and in the army absolutely, seniority is the clinching argument, and that bloody freshmen should hold their tongues.

A striking difference between the air of Balliol and the air of Eton was that at Balliol the atmosphere was free from any taint of athlete-worship. This could not have been said of all Colleges in those days; in many of them 'Blues' were all but adored, and the famous

B

Jack Raphael strolled about the town attended by his courtiers. Balliol expected, and achieved, a more adult outlook in her young men. There was plenty of keenness, especially at Rugger and on the river, but success in games added nothing to a man's popularity or consideration inside the College gates. This tradition enabled the wit, the scholar, the musician or the eccentric, whose growth at school had been retarded by obscurity, like that of plants kept in a cellar, to blossom and to expand. In the shifting groups that knotted or untied themselves beneath the elms and chestnut trees of the Quad, the central figure may have sometimes worn an Annandale, but rarely a dark blue, tie.

That there were cliques is undeniable. The Dons, bravely aiming at the impossible, did their best to discountenance them, and I suppose that in an ideal College, as in an ideal world, all men would be brothers. But you cannot make friends to order, and in day-to-day living, cliques are as inevitable as they are agreeable. Among the first of freedoms is that of choosing one's cronies, and the man who likes everybody has neither palate for the spice of friendship, nor flavour for his friends.

The accident of my having lodged, as a freshman, on Number XIV staircase gave me easy access to the 'Anna' set — the members of the Annandale Society. Theoretically a debating, but practically a dining, Club, the 'Anna' regarded itself with complacence, to say the least. No athletic or academic qualifications were required for admission. High spirits, humour, sociability, easy manners and the right pronunciation of 'shibboleth' were all that was necessary. If the Society had in

my generation a distinctly Etonian flavour, it was but
a flavour, and P. T. Lewis of South Africa, Raoul de
Liedekerke from Belgium, Louis de Gramont from
France and de Witt Hutchings of Princeton were
prominent and popular members. To the Dons the
'Anna' was a perennial problem. On the one hand, it
was a clique which appeared, on occasions, to 'own'
the College in the most blatant fashion, and on the night
of the 'Anna' dinner was both noisy and destructive.
On the other hand, the members of the 'Anna' were
among those undergraduates whom the Dons loved
best, and were as hard-working and as serious-minded,
at the proper times, as any Don could wish. If they
destroyed large quantities of College crockery in those
delectable 'waterfalls' which went crashing down the
turret staircases, and on a grander scale, down the steps
of Hall itself, they paid the bill next morning punctually
and cheerfully. If they drank a great deal of Pol Roger
'98 at their dinners in the Junior Common Room, and
disturbed the studious and the obscure with 'The more
we drink together', 'The Workhouse Master', 'Evviva
la Siena', 'The Dutch Companee' or 'Gordouli', they
had brought to perfection the art of becoming 'buffy'
without drunkenness. I have never discovered the
literary, non-colloquial word to describe the condition
of 'buffiness', but to achieve it with precision is to have
mastered a profitable technique in the art of living. For
it is the point where wine 'maketh glad the heart of
man', liberating his spirit from the fears, inhibitions
and shynesses which so often clog social intercourse
between water-drinkers, but stopping well short of loss
of self-control. 'Buffiness' breaks out into song and
dance ; promotes reconciliations ; dissolves prejudices ;

is positive, hopeful and affirmative, and leads on to high jinks. It is most enjoyable.

Unfortunately, except on such an occasion as a Bump Supper, the whole College did not become buffy at one and the same time. The high jinks that amused the Annandale Society after dinner did not always amuse the studious abstainers who found themselves suddenly involved in the fun. There was the case of Moonface. It was part of the ritual, before the waterfalls began, to climb the turret stairs to the high room where Moonface was certain to be found at his books, and to worship him. The multi-coloured representatives of the Sovereign States belonging to the United Nations may or may not have detected, beneath the grave urbanity of Sir Alexander Cadogan, a tendency to Moonface-worship. But worship Moonface he did, as chief officiating priest, and upon his knees. 'O Moonface . . .' The allocution was solemn, reverent and highly complimentary to the worshipped. But no flicker of amusement relieved the solemnity of Moonface's large, white, perfectly circular countenance. He sat and gazed down at his kneeling adorers, patient, immobile and unamused. It is probable that he felt not so much contempt as utter incomprehension. For Norman Campbell was a dedicated man ; dedicated partly to scientific research, but wholly to the succour of the poor and the weak. Mock-worship of such a man, so retiring that his moonface was all that we knew about him, was not a happy occasion for making further acquaintance ; and most of us missed our chance of getting to know a remarkable human being, probably worth more than the rest of us added together. For Moonface went from Balliol to teach science at Trinity

College, Kandy, and to combine, with his teaching, such other activities that when a missionary was telling the people of a neighbouring village about the life and character of Jesus, they stopped him. 'We know him,' they said, 'he lives at Trinity College.' When war broke out, Moonface returned to fight and was killed at Arras in 1917.

What sort of men were the Dons, precisely fifty years ago, who, winking with misgivings at the noises and breakages of 'Anna' nights, gave to Balliol its strongly individual flavour, and how did they do it? The Master, Edward Caird, was little known to us. A Scottish philosopher of international reputation, who had been chosen to succeed Jowett over the head of the Senior Fellow, the much-loved J. L. Strachan-Davidson, he was now old, ill, shy and retiring. There was a story current in my day of his encounter with a nervous freshman who had been asked to breakfast. The freshman arrived early, and found the Master alone upon the hearthrug, looking like a Father Christmas who was afraid of children. Conversation languished. The Master turned to the bow-window that overlooks the chestnut tree and the Quad. 'We have a little sun this morning,' he remarked, in his good Scots accent. 'C—congratulations, sir,' said the ingenuous young man, 'and how is Mrs. Caird?' Mrs. Caird was as well as can be expected at eighty. But for most of us, contact with this distinguished old man was limited to receiving from his hands in Hall, where he sat motionless as the Buddha, our weekly battels, or to hearing him render a famous line from the *Odyssey* as 'I would preferr to be an agricooltural labourerr all my days . . .'.

It is a measure of Caird's remoteness from, and Strachan-Davidson's lively impact upon, us undergraduates, that I have for many years past been prepared to swear that Caird retired during my second term, and that Strachan-Davidson reigned as Master during the remainder of my four years at Oxford. On consulting reference books, I find that, on the contrary, Caird was Master during the whole of my time at Balliol except for the last summer term. Strachan-Davidson was in fact the Dean, but so effectually the head and front of the College that memory, sometimes more truthful than mere facts, has bestowed on him the office which he held in all but name.

To those who never knew 'Strachan' in the flesh, it is difficult to justify in words the extraordinary hold he had upon the imaginations and affections of many of us. He said and did no memorable things, like Jowett; he did not make the name of Master of Balliol illustrious outside her walls, like A. L. Smith; he was not a reformer, a moralist, or a champion of causes, like A. D. Lindsay. His learning, deep in his own subject of Roman Law, was not wide, and he was not an inspiring lecturer. Although he had the gift, when talking to one or two in his own rooms, of making his Roman friends, and especially Cicero, come alive, yet even in this gift for seeing certain Romans as contemporaries he was surpassed by his friend Warde Fowler. He had no speculative turn of mind; religion or the tremendous paradoxes of existence were never discussed by Strachan. He did not stimulate us to mental adventure, or to put awkward questions to God: he was conservative in opinion, liberal in sympathies, single-minded in his pursuit, which was the honour and welfare of the

College.   Fine of feature, kindly of eye, tall with the
stoop of delicacy, he walked among us familiarly beneath the trees or, waistcoat unbuttoned, poured tea for
us in the companionable disorder of his study.   He was
simple and even humble, for all his invincible dignity,
and while patently a great gentleman, it is not easy to
explain why, with so many limitations, he was, for so
many of us, *the* Master of our lifetimes.   It was not
just that his native courtesy and fine manners enlarged
our self-esteem, for Strachan made us humble where
A. L. Smith inspired self-reliance.   Perhaps the secret of
his appeal to us was that we recognised in the Master
virtue that appeared imitable, if by no means attainable,
by those of us lacking intellectual distinction.   We all
knew how, after twenty years as Senior Fellow, he had
been denied his dearest ambition in favour of Caird,
and with what magnanimity and generosity he had
welcomed and served his supplanter.   I cannot be the
only Balliol man who became, through Strachan's
example, immune to that virus that sometimes attacks
us lifelong players of second fiddles.   And a man for
whom loyalty and unselfseeking are not merits but a
matter of course does not govern young men for
nothing.   From one point of view, I am not sure that
Strachan's influence and example was wholly satisfactory.   A sense of duty goes far, but it does not carry
a man all the way to public service on the grand scale.
Ambition is also needed to drive the reluctant spirit
through the horrors of political life.   And in the face
of Strachan's simplicity ambition was apt to wither.
Nor did he give us, as Jowett seems to have given to
the young Asquith and the other Balliol men of his
day, a 'tranquil consciousness of effortless superiority'.

Strachan, rolling his own cigarettes from the tobacco
he kept in a pouch as big as a handbag, and discoursing,
with 'er—er—er' between every few words, to young
gentlemen whose names he could rarely, if ever,
remember, did not make us feel superior. He made us
his humble servants ; and because the Master put the
College first, we, as became his humble servants, tried,
in our small ways, to do the same.

A. L. Smith, who succeeded Strachan first as Dean
and then as Master, was wholly unlike, physically and
mentally, the old-fashioned, hesitant Strachan, who
rode over Shotover on horseback and could only tell
us apart by the help of such mnemonics as 'Tea-pot'
or 'Little Black Dog' in the margin of his College List.
Ardent, robust and warm-hearted, 'A. L.' appeared to
know us all by character as well as by sight. He was
square and sunburnt and a little rugged, and believed
that what young men need is, above all things, encouragement. He was a great teacher of history, after the
school of F. W. Maitland. He knew how to arouse
our curiosity through the thoughts of some obscure
thirteenth-century monk ; he could persuade us that
the village muck-heap was of greater moment to our
ancestors than the quarrels of kings. He would stand at a
table and shuffle the ink-pot and pieces of pink blotting-
paper until you saw with your eyes the ambitions of
the Emperor Frederick II. He commanded me, before
an Easter vacation, to spend half of it in the British
Museum with a German book on the Middle Ages.

'But I don't read German, sir.'

'I only want you to read the Latin quotations in the
footnotes.'

'I'm very bad at Latin, sir.'

'This is dog-Latin — anybody can read it !'

He was right. The Latin was of the kind I had myself written in Fourth Form, and the quotations, carefully memorised, came in most handily in Schools.

'A. L.' must have been as tough as leather. He was always playing hockey or rowing in skilled company. Yet he found time for vigorous activities in the W.E.A. ; Balliol, he thought, belonged to the country, not to Balliol men alone. Where Strachan saw the College as a magnet drawing the young *élite* to itself, 'A. L.' saw it as a sprinkler, watering dry places beyond the College walls. Self-civilisation, the aim of most of us who took Oxford seriously, was not enough for him. We must, he held, go out and civilise the outsider. But to sprinkle effectively you must have a full tank, and 'A. L.' saw that Balliol Dons could not be expected to live on prestige and devotion alone. So he talked to two rich Balliol men as only he knew how to talk, and the result was an Endowment Fund, and a living stipend for the Fellows, with increases for long service. Lord Brassey and Lord Newlands deserve well of Balliol ; but it was 'A. L.' who 'touched' them, in both senses of the word.

'A. L.', who was never in a hurry except when walking, found time to bring up a family of two sons and seven daughters, all endowed with beauty or brains or both. When I went up to Balliol as a freshman, the daughters were still at home, and 'the King's Mound', where they lived, was a name vibrant with overtones. To some of us it meant Gertrude under the apple-blossom, too pretty to be quite true. Gertrude could afford to be warm and welcoming, because she was engaged to Harold Hartley, one of the younger Dons, and so could not be suspected of flirting. To be above suspicion is of great advantage to a pretty young woman, and hardly less so to her youthful admirers. It was the fashion among some of my contemporaries to pretend that Gertrude was being thrown away on Harold Hartley, whose quiet, shy manners seemed to them ill-fitted to his situation as Gertrude's fiancé. They hinted that, in his shoes, they would have blown trumpets and waved banners all day. I am not sure that Archie Gordon did not even dream of a cutting-out expedition. I was not one of the deceived. I could not have then foreseen the extraordinary adventure, courage, versatility and public service of Brigadier Sir Harold Hartley's subsequent career. But I did know by instinct that he was a better man than we were, and that Gertrude was to be worthily mated. This is not the place to speak of the living, but for me 'the King's Mound' recalls, gratefully, the beginnings of a lifelong friendship, warmed by admiration. But to some others the King's Mound had a formidable aspect. 'A. L.', in his hospitable way, used to invite the crews of the Torpids to supper. Between each shy oarsman sat a daughter. If you sat next to Gertrude you were saved ; but Molly, no less ravishingly pretty, was gestating a First Class in History, and fear of her intellect prevented many a spotty young man from savouring to the full the sight of the curls that clustered so bewitchingly about her nape. If you sent up a lob in talk, her return was killing. The younger girls sat silent, considering their verdict. To judge from their expressions, it was 'guilty but insane'. Biddy, the poetess, hieratic in appearance as Dame Edith Sitwell, alone brooded unconscious of our presence.

Over all presided Mrs. A. L. Smith, like a faintly mischievous Madonna. That golden-hearted woman was not good at pretending. She did not like raw young men, and though willing, for 'A. L.'s' sake, to feed them generously, she saw no reason to put them at their ease. They, for their part, were too gauche to tell her what cried out for telling, that she had a lovely face. That it would have worked I know, for I tried it early, and never looked back. But she was a rarity, a collector's piece, and freshmen rowing in the Torpids are not, as a rule, connoisseurs of human beings as valuable as was Mrs. A. L. And since her feelings, backed by a sevenfold Amen in the eyes of the silent jury-daughters, were not hidden from her young guests, those suppers were not looked forward to by entertainers or entertained. All the same, the daughters may not have wasted their time. For a few years later they picked husbands, one by one, with unerring eyes for quality and promise. Those embarrassing evenings of silent observation must have taught them, at least, the art of discarding. 'A. L.' lived to assemble round his table a set of sons-in-law worthy of himself and his family, and well capable of assaying the gold-content of his wife. She, in turn, had no longer anything to be bad at pretending about, and the King's Mound, in after years, could be approached by the shyest without a preliminary wiping of damp palms.

On more than one occasion of success or of disappointment I was to find upon my table a note from 'A. L.', in a thin, spidery script, of applause or consolation. I wonder to this day at the good-heartedness of a man who, cumbered and preoccupied, could find time to minister to the feelings of a single

undergraduate. And when, in my last year, I became
his pupil, he made a point of taking me *tête-à-tête* three
times a week for an hour or more including part of
the Christmas vacation. Such expenditure of time and
trouble upon individuals was part of the Balliol tradition, and any man with an outside chance of a First
Class in Schools was given this attention as a matter of
course by the younger Dons, but 'A. L.' at this time
was the Dean, no longer young, harassed with University as well as College business, and knew that I was
already being given 'solo' hours by H. W. C. Davis,
the redoubtable 'Fluffy'.

When I recollect his manifold kindness to myself, as
well as the fascination of his conversation, wise, witty
and far-ranging, and the way that in later years, when
I had the honour to belong to 'the Club', we used to
jockey for positions on entering the dining-room, fear-
ing to be seated out of ear-shot from 'A. L.', I wonder
how it is that, for me, Strachan-Davidson is still *the*
Master of my experience. Perhaps it is that 'A. L.' had
one weakness — that of thinking all his geese to be
swans. A goose, taken for a swan and well aware of
the mistake, suffers from a sense of strain : over-
encouragement can even turn to discouragement such
as my own when it was reported to me that Grant
Robertson, an influential Fellow of All Souls, had said :
'I hear the Dean of Balliol has already elected our
History Fellow for us, *but we shall see*'. They did see ;
and I was beaten for All Souls by an all-round better
man, and had no complaints, but the memory of Grant
Robertson's words did not comfort me as I sat in All
Souls Hall, beneath the glint of Grant Robertson's
glasses, conning the papers by which the supreme

ambition of my life was to be achieved or missed. I
think, looking back, that I was always trying to live
up to 'A. L.'s' expectations and to justify the warm
personal interest which this big-hearted man took in all
of his pupils, and that, conscious of falling short of his
hopes, I shared in the goose's embarrassment.

From Strachan-Davidson there was no such pressure
to excel. He took us as we were, giving us his confidence without demanding more in return than was
in us. There was something in 'Strachan' of the
Countess Rosmarin in Christopher Fry's play :

> You know . . . how apparently undemandingly
> She moves among us ; and yet
> Lives make and unmake themselves in her neighbourhood
> As nowhere else.

He exerted his influence solely by what he was in himself. For the many who needed, and responded to,
bracing, 'A. L.' was the man : but from me 'Strachan',
who asked nothing, drew all the devotion I had to give.
And it is devotion, not gratitude and admiration, that
in the last resort elects, for each of us, *the* Master of our
memories.

'Fluffy' Davis, unlike 'A. L.', was a difficult man to
know. When a colleague, 'Jimmy' Palmer, in an un-
guarded moment in Senior Common Room, once called
him 'Fluffy', he was downed with 'Are you addressing
me, Palmer ?' and it was a very foolish young man
indeed who, summoned to the Junior Dean's rooms to
answer for a drunken frolic, made an attempt to pass it
off as between men of the world : 'I say, Fluffy — I'm
afraid I made rather a floater last night.' Davis had
light-blue eyes, cold and unwavering as pebbles behind
his glasses. 'If by "Fluffy" you mean me, my name is

Mr. Davis ; and if by "floater" you mean making a beast of yourself, I heartily concur.' But behind the rigidity and reserve of this shy and learned man there was ardour and sensitivity and warmth. Few can have known of the hopeless romance and of the bitter-sweet influence of a 'Princesse Lointaine', which for several years brought shine and shadow to his hidden, disciplined heart. He was not an imaginative historian ; he did not eavesdrop, like a G. M. Young, among his Angevins and hear them talk, or recoil from the stench of their insanitary strongholds ; but he could collect and weigh and marshal evidence, and had an uncanny insight into the minds of examiners. He liked the badges of success, and had no first-aid to give to those who got Second Classes. But he was unexpectedly human over good food and wine, and his kindness was constant, for he was wholly unselfish. In a College where the Senior Fellows were all but demigods, and the younger Fellows only just not companions, there was, I think, a place for this single-minded devotee of education in its purely academic sense. His very aloofness from games and athletics, and even from those desultory discussions where legs hang over the arms of chairs, conferred upon him a kind of authority. He was our frosty weather ; his high standards and cold integrity nipped, but braced, us all.

Of the other Senior Fellows, Pickard-Cambridge and the Baron de Paravicini were classical scholars with whom, as a 'Pass Mods' man, I had no contact, and only those old Balliol men who were scholars enough to do justice to 'Paravi's' learning have a right to tell the story of Paravi at Parson's Pleasure, and even then not in print. But J. A. Smith, later Professor of Moral

Philosophy, held mild and melancholy sway over the unformed minds of all Greats men. This large, soft-spoken, untidy Scot, with a drooping moustache and unsmiling eyes, had an almost priestly attitude to the philosophy he taught us. His belief in 'the Absolute' was as living and reverent as a Christian's belief in God, and he regarded Pragmatists with the horror felt by a Newman for a Colenso. His faith did not, however, fortify him against the minor ills of life, and he was anything but a 'philosopher' in the popular, everyday sense of the word. A cold in the head was, for poor 'J. A.', a disaster, and his melancholy was often supposed, rightly or wrongly, to be that of the love-lorn. It was hard on him to be middle-aged and a trifle moth-eaten when the girls at the King's Mound were so pretty ; but we sometimes felt, with the cruelty of youth, that a great philosopher should have had readier access to the higher consolations. For all that, when we sat in his girl-forsaken rooms, and heard him expound metaphysics in his slow, meandering sentences, that were invariably accompanied by the movement of a forefinger weaving arabesques upon the uppermost knee of his crossed legs, we knew that we were privileged. For his mind was large and lucid, and his passionate belief in the relevance of philosophy to behaviour almost compelled us to regard Greats as a training for life as much as for a good class in Schools. It was a belief fully shared by his understudy and fellow Scot, the young A. D. Lindsay, for whom Immanuel Kant was a prophet and torch-bearer ; and it is humiliating to have to confess that, with two such teachers, I was never able, try as I might, to apply metaphysics to life or to what I, unlike Kant, took for 'reality'. I enjoyed my attempts to crack the hard nuts of the *Critique of Pure Reason*, but only as a kind of strenuous game, and it was the same with all the metaphysicians, from Plato downward. Logic was different, for it supplied one with weapons for use ; and the study of moral philosophy at least had the important practical effect of throwing one back, once and for all, upon Conscience. But metaphysics, if they are to be more than a mental pastime, must in the end be equated with Theology — and Theology can never be more than speculation about the Unknowable. It can tell us nothing about what *is* ; its affirmations can only be about what men at various times and in various places have imagined.

In middle-age I came across an old notebook containing my Greats essays, and read one called 'The Nature of Truth'. I could not understand a word of it. Elderly, I have been equally baffled by an attempt to grasp Logical Positivism, which has, I understand, cut the ground from under all the traditional philosophies. This incapacity to understand, in middle and late life, the kind of thinking and the kind of language which were intelligible, albeit with an effort, to myself at twenty-two would be disheartening indeed if I had shared the faith of my teachers in the validity of what they taught. I am able to keep up my spirits in spite of this evidence of mental decay, which in my own case set in unusually early, largely because I regarded the whole thing as a great game. One is sorry when one can no longer row, but one is not humiliated, for rowing is but a sport. And to me the study of such philosophies as were taught fifty years ago was a magnificent exercise for the mind, and nothing more.

This is not to say that I think we wasted our time over Greats. The development and exercise of our capacities for clear thinking are, I suppose, important ends of higher education, and for those congenitally incapable of mathematical reasoning, the study of logic and of the more obscure metaphysicians is a fine, tough, exacting employment. That we enjoyed it is proved by the midnight arguments among ourselves, over whisky and 'togger' cake ; not entirely sham fights, either, for it must not be supposed that the ardent faith of our 'J. A.s' and A. D. Lindsays made no converts.

Philosophy being an attempt to penetrate through appearance to reality, it might be expected, by a visitor from, say, China or Mars, that the College Chaplain would be the man most deeply involved in its exposition and discussion, since God, if He exists, must be the essence of what we mean by 'reality'. Such a visitor would have been naïve indeed. Our chaplain, 'Jimmy' Palmer (who afterwards won renown as Bishop of Bombay and was reputed to have 'dominated' a Lambeth Conference), taught us Formal Logic, and what is meant by the 'Undistributed Middle'. Bearded, pithy, tactless, amusing and amused, he bore most courageously with a stammer that was later to condemn his luckless wife to be known throughout India as 'the Baboon' since, on a public occasion, Jimmy had referred to her as 'the greatest b—b—b—b—boon in my life'. But the idea that Jimmy, through being in Holy Orders, could have contributed anything to our knowledge of ultimate reality never entered our heads. Had he not publicly declared at his Ordination that he unfeignedly believed all the Canonical Scriptures of the Old as well as of the New Testament, thereby identifying the

c

terrible Yahveh with God ? Did he not profess a creed
that imputes to the very Source of all goodness a 'plan
of salvation' both arbitrary and unjust ? In the speculative climate of Balliol fifty years ago these were
disabling handicaps indeed. We went to Chapel very
willingly, but held ourselves free to ignore Creeds
where they clashed with Conscience. Had Jimmy been
a Rashdall Hastings it might well have been different.
But in that case he could never have become a Bishop.
Today, in a world so shocked that it can even supply
adherents to the cosmic despair of a Karl Barth, I am
told that most Oxford Colleges (but not Balliol) have
chaplains in whose eyes Jimmy would have been almost
a free-thinker. Humanity having made such a fool of
itself, say the chaplains, it must now give up thinking
and 'believe'. But it was not the wrong thinking of
humanity, it was Hitler and a few other wicked men
that all but wrecked civilisation ; and the Creed for
which the chaplains stand is itself no more than the
fossilised thoughts of a handful of men in a fractional
period of humanity's history. That 'the Kingdom of
Heaven is within you' remains, and must needs remain,
true, for without that divine spark which is Conscience
men could not have conceived of a Kingdom of Heaven,
let alone hope to achieve it. But Conscience does not
develop under authority, but in freedom, and, in particular, must be matured and toughened by having to
pit itself against Reason. So that it was not Jimmy's
professional affirmations, but the cut-and-thrust in our
own or Cyril Bailey's fire-lit rooms, or even under the
stars on summer nights, that taught us to find our moral
legs. For young men, luckily, take their souls seriously,
and, if metaphysics was to many of us a game, our

search for a scale of values, acceptable by reason and conscience alike, was anything but a sham.

Daily attendance at Chapel was not compulsory at Balliol ; it was enough, instead, to answer to your name at a roll-call held in the College porch. For this, cap and gown had to be worn, but beneath them, at any rate in winter, a great-coat could conceal the lack of much, and 'a dirty Roller' could be done in very few minutes indeed. And then, back to bed. But on Sundays it was the thing to go to Chapel once at any rate, and we went with a good will. The interior of Balliol Chapel in those days was lamentable to the eyes, and there was no visible source of the spell these short and austere services cast over some of us. But, for all our cliques, there was a latent but strong sense of unity in the College, and, worship or not Whom we might there, we came out of Chapel less divided, less self-occupied and more tolerant than we went in. Some unseen Hand in that unlovely place could draw us, imperceptibly, to a centre.

And years later, towards the end of the first Great War, when I was ill, severely wounded, half-starved, sleepless and a prisoner of war among the sands of Pomerania, it was Balliol Chapel that rendered me first-aid in a curious way. For when my attention had wandered during Jimmy's or Henry Gibbon's sermons, I had been used to read the memorial tablets on the Chapel walls. There was one of these set up to the joint memory of Evelyn Abbott and Sir John Conroy, at the foot of which was inscribed, in Greek, a passage, not from the Gospels, but from — of all unlikely authors — Aristotle. I knew just enough Greek to construe it after a fashion, and it was in Greek that I memorised it, and in Greek that I repeated it to myself for comfort in my troubles. An English version might be as follows :

> Even so something fine shows through, when a man bears his misfortunes gently, many and grievous though they be, not from lack of feeling, but because of the stuff he is made of and his own proud soul.

To some, no doubt, it will seem almost shocking that Balliol Chapel should have sent a message to a Balliol man in distress through the words of a pagan writer. But so it was ; and it worked.

One Don who did not go to Chapel was Francis Urquhart — familiar, and endeared, to all Balliol men as 'Sligger'. For 'Sligger' was a devout Roman Catholic, loyal to, but never speaking of, the faith in which he was born. His bearing through many years as a teacher of young men is a clinching answer to those Protestants who pretend that no Roman Catholic in daily commerce with youth can refrain from some measure, however discreet, of propaganda for 'the Faith'. Not even as a teacher of history did he betray any bias in favour of Rome. He was as judicial as an Acland, and had as much reverence for facts as a C. P. Scott. It was the fashion, in my time, to decry Urquhart as a teacher of history. It was true that he had to stand comparison with A. L. Smith and H. W. C. Davis, both outstanding historians. But, having been allotted to 'Sligger' for a few weeks when my own tutor was out of action, I was deeply impressed by him. It may have been due to my own ignorance, but he seemed to me to get under the skin of the men for whom the Middle Ages were modern times, and to take his pupil with him. It was, at any rate, a stimulating experience, and I should have liked to prolong it.

But 'Sligger's' main rôle at Balliol was social, not pedagogic. Cherubic, pouting, with thick curly hair and slight, athletic limbs, he appeared to have endless leisure for loitering in the Quad by day and gossiping in his rooms by night. He never said or did anything remarkable, but we took comfort in his company and felt the better for it. His was the function of a catalyst, to liberate in others their latent capacities for fusion. In 'Sligger's' rooms, the Annandale characters from Number XIV staircase met the Blundell's scholars and the shy, lone freshman who lived high in a turret of the Front Quad. Beneath Edward Lear's precise, surprising paintings of the Holy Land, or flanking the chimney-piece whence the photographs of bygone Balliol men stared in close order, we lounged and swung our legs and munched cake and drank whisky or tea ; while 'Sligger' threw the ball, not to those who were best at catching, but to those whose turn to catch it, at home or at school, had been lost or forgotten altogether.

From an enforced delicacy about paying for the long journey to Chamonix, I never made one of 'Sligger's' celebrated 'Chalet parties', and am for that reason disqualified from painting him in the round. And there is the further difficulty, that 'Sligger', like Strachan-Davidson, did his part in civilising us by being what he was, not by sayings or doings. He bowled with us at the nets, he dined with us at Vincent's or the Grid, he came punting on the Cherwell, or walked with us, in Sunday pepper-and-salt suits, over Shotover, but, equal and companionable as he was, he never lived on our level. He had his own interior to mind ; a secret chamber that had to be most scrupulously swept and garnished ; and we felt this and, without envying, admired. It was not just his ascetiicsm that set him apart, his contempt for great-coats when the wind was easterly, his lack of interest in food and drink, his early Masses and comfortless bedroom. It was rather a kind of selfless humility, a casual and quotidian air of sauntering because who was he to set himself above saunterers ?

Since this friendly man, with a touch of the friar alike in his looks and his ubiquity, attached to himself, for all his unexciting simplicity, the greater part of the College, it is clear that the Balliol of my days was no longer the Balliol of Jowett. It is difficult to imagine a Henry Asquith or a George Curzon at a Chalet party, or even condescending to the pleasant causeries in 'Sligger's' rooms of an evening. Were we less sure of ourselves, less ambitious, or simply less strenuous than our predecessors in the great Jowett period in which Balliol, the oldest College of all, had flowered at length after waiting seven hundred years ? I do not think so. We still led the field in Schools. We still won the Ireland, the Craven and the Hertford. We still regarded ourselves, in our corporate capacity, as one of three great educational institutions : Balliol, Oxford and Cambridge. But I believe it to be true of us, as in-dividuals, that we did take ourselves less seriously than the scholastic generation before us, just as they took themselves less seriously than did the young Gladstones or Hallams of earlier days still. And I am certain that it is true of the Dons. It was not only 'Sligger' who closed the gap between tutor and undergraduate. Harold Hartley, Cyril Bailey and, a little later, Sandie Lindsay, all helped to initiate or maintain a tradition, which has persisted to this day, of easy and familiar commerce between the younger Dons and the undergraduates. And when a tutor condescends to meet his juniors on these terms, allowing himself to be called by his Christian name (or, as in 'Sligger's' case, by a grotesque nickname), he is deliberately risking a loss of prestige. He is exposing his mind, not when it is keyed up for lecturing or tuition, but when it is relaxed and frequently fatigued. He is exhibiting his character, tastes and values, not as becoming a Balliol Don, but as they are in his unbuttoned, fireside moods. That these young Fellows of the College did in fact lose no prestige, but won, through intimacy, our affection as well as our respect, is a tribute to the kind of men they were, and a proof of the success of the system. But it did, I believe, change the College 'ethos' from one of preoccupation with intellect to one of concern for personal relationships. In an Italian newspaper, about the period of which I am writing, there appeared a sketch of Mr. Asquith's career. Of Balliol the writer remarked : 'Balliol è l'atrofia del cuore, ma o ! che cervelli !' In our day Balliol was anything but the atrophy of the heart, although brains may still have been in the 'oh !' class.

The case of Cyril Bailey is in point. This distinguished scholar, famed Public Orator and translator and editor of Lucretius, is still very much alive, and, to save his modesty, I must try to forget gratitude and affection. In my day at Balliol, 'Cyril', as we all called him, shared with a slightly Senior Fellow the task of seeing that Balliol's name occurred more often than that of any other College in the list of Firsts in Honour Mods ; and that such prizes as the Hertford,

Craven and Ireland Scholarships should only occasionally, and just to keep up the competitive spirit, fall to
outsiders. In this task he was pre-eminently successful.
But I cannot help thinking that he did even better work
as friend, confidant and mentor to many of us who,
having little Latin and less Greek, were never his pupils.
Much as he liked scholars, he liked human beings better
still, and, feeling his way cautiously and always with
humour, admitted us by degrees to a private view of
his own fine and fastidious values. A devoted friend
of 'Sligger's', he supplemented 'Sligger's' comfortable
but slightly pedestrian hob-nobbing with his own
sharper tang. Personally, I owe to him the first introduction to both classical music and painting, two lifelong pleasures, and a habit of regarding aesthetics less
as a pursuit or a hobby than as an integral part of living.
He educated us, unconsciously, in his moments of ease;
but that he was enabled to do so is due to his willingness,
with the other younger Fellows, to incur all the risks of
intimacy. His colleague, who kept aloof from all but
his own pupils, undoubtedly contributed to their success
in the Schools and to the College's consequent renown,
but for the rest of us he was non-existent. There can be
no question as to which of them did the better job.

Most of this out-of-school, casual, heart-to-heart
method of educating and civilising us took place in the
Dons' rooms at night, with drinks and tobacco, and it
was little wonder that 'Strachan' regarded the marriage
of a junior Fellow as an act almost amounting to dis-
loyalty to the College. And it must be admitted that
the Balliol system does depend upon the younger
Fellows living in College, and not in North Oxford
with perambulators blocking the entrance-hall. Ideally,

a Balliol Fellowship should be a vocation, like the Roman Catholic priesthood, demanding vows of celibacy, at any rate for a long term of years. Nowadays, the social climate seems less favourable than formerly to the vocation and preservation of bachelor Dons. Are the new Women's Colleges flooding our courts and quadrangles with nubile and Don-loving girls to blame ? Or is it just the new freedom and comradeship between the sexes, with the greatly extended pool of interests and pursuits common to both, that discourages celibacy ? It is certain that, fifty years ago, girls were out of the picture at Oxford, except in Eights Week and at Commemoration Balls. Relations with them were formal and mannered, a prescribed distance was kept, and topics for talk limited. Pretty girls were idealised beyond their deserts, plain ones were pitied beyond their needs, and the notional gap between man and girl made it difficult for either to regard the other as a simple fellow-creature. So that in those days a young man with intellectual interests, living the collegiate life, had a good chance of dodging Nature, if only through lack of opportunity, for many years on end ; and a very good thing for the College it was. If the younger Fellows of today succumb more readily to matrimony, the fault is hardly theirs. Girls have become so pervasive and approachable that even married undergraduates are not uncommon, and a young Don has every excuse for arguing with himself that if he is to devote himself to the College, he must first abate the restiveness of a normal male unmated in a world of accessible and on-coming young women. It is the argument used for centuries by the marrying clergy, Protestant or Russian Orthodox. But that it can be resisted has been proved, and, while the last person capable of joining such a Resistance Movement, I shall go on thinking, with Strachan, that Balliol is best served when she is sole mistress of a young Don's heart. The cases of Harold Hartley in the years in question, and of Kenneth Bell in a later generation, will be cited against me ; and indeed few Fellows of the College have ever taken so many burdens upon their own shoulders or been better friends and guides to Balliol men, than these two youthful husbands. But Harold and Kenneth were exceptions to all rules ; their vitality and, in Hartley's case, versatility were *hors concours*. I rule their cases out as irrelevant : they were portents, not samples.

The youngest Fellow to leave his mark upon the men of my own years was A. D. Lindsay. He was the son of that Principal Lindsay whose correspondence with Janet Ross, Queen of Florence and hammer of 'Ouida', might have cured the Scotophobia of a Johnson. My first recollection of Sandie was being shown by him reviews by two Scottish newspapers of Principal Lindsay's volumes, which had lately appeared, on the Reformation. The author had quoted with approval somebody's remark that 'Erasmus looks, in his portraits, as if he had been descended from a long line of maiden aunts'. Both reviewers had seized upon this passage for comment. The one, remarking that the author had 'slipped' for once, felt sure that on reflection Principal Lindsay would see that such a descent would have been impossible. The other, while expressing scepticism, added that 'if true, what a light it threw upon the morality of the times !'

Lindsay coached us in philosophy for Greats, and took a few of us upon an Easter reading-party to

Dartmoor. He completely won our hearts. Austerely
bred, a moralist, reformer and egalitarian, with a prejudice almost amounting to dislike against English
Public Schools, his fairness, good humour and lively
sense of fun made him a delightful companion. He
was the first complete Scot we had ever met ; a thin,
porridge-eating, argumentative, religious, metaphysical
Know-all ; but his sense of humour never failed, and
he saw himself much as we saw him. He came as near,
I believe, to having the 'giftie' Robbie Burns prayed
for as any man I have known ; and it gave him his
self-confidence as well as his simplicity. We guessed
at greatness in him, even then ; but not, owing to his
native good manners, at his dislike of some of our
friends. It was indeed only many years later that I
was to learn how his democratic soul loathed the
masterful, nonchalant airs (which he called 'hubris')
of the Annandale set to which we belonged. Lindsay
was a thorough-going 'under-dogger' all his life, and
hated to see Julian Grenfell chasing young Philip Sassoon
out of College with a stock-whip. But, leveller as he
was, he was always insistent that levelling must be
upwards, not downwards. He wanted equality of
opportunity, but no lowering of standards. The
Elementary schoolboy should have a pathway to
Balliol, but, to arrive, he must be fully equipped. And
Lindsay's standards were high indeed.

These, then, were the Fellows of Balliol fifty years
ago, who in some ways maintained, in others greatly
modified, the Jowett tradition. They maintained it
on the purely academic side by the system of giving
personal attention, through *tête-à-tête* sessions, to all
men of promise. They changed it — and in this the

Hartleys, Urquharts, Baileys and Lindsays must have most of the credit, under the pervasive humanity of Strachan-Davidson and 'A. L.' — by a new emphasis upon personal relationships and the art of living. We were taught, I believe, by these men to develop all our inner resources, as well as our mental powers ; to look about us, to despise mere convention, to judge for ourselves, to cross-examine authority, to demand proofs, to make no claims and, above all, to enjoy. I believe that, but for the first Great War, my own generation of Balliol men would have walked the world with a different sort of reputation from that of 'effortless superiority'. They might even have become distinguishable by their freedom from pretensions.

But these devoted Dons of whom I have written had, in a few years, to see their work largely thrown away. For the mortality among Balliol men in the first Great War was great, and many of those who survived had much of the stuffing knocked out of them. It was the pick of us who died ; the stamp of Balliol upon the rest of us can hardly have been noticed. On the other hand, the tradition in the College has been carried on. Men who came under the influence of a Kenneth Bell, a Humphrey Sumner, a Roger Mynors — to name only a few — are, I can hardly doubt, going about with the same inner security and unpretentious bearing as their forerunners who fell in battle. But they, too, are tragically fewer since Hitler's war. Is 'a Balliol man' a recognised type nowadays ? Probably not, in the world at large. But to Balliol men themselves, in secret and in private conclave with their fellows, there is no doubt as to what a 'Balliol man' stands for. But we do well to keep it to ourselves.

II

I HAVE sometimes thought that the life we led at Balliol half a century ago was a pattern, in miniature, of what a civilised western community ought to provide for us all. A sane view of procreation could, in the long run, assure that the population should have as much elbow-room within the national borders as we enjoyed in the Quad, on the river, in the Master's Field and on our Sunday walks over Boar's Hill or Shotover. Atomic power, applied to housekeeping, would take the place of our parents in paying our tuition fees and battels. Those who are always happier working with their hands than with their heads would represent the faithful College Scouts. Combativeness would have its outlet, as we had ours, in games, not war. Our leaders would be, not politicians, but those who could show us the best sport, mental or physical, and be pre-eminent, above all, in the art of living.

For in those roomy, uncrowded years we did indeed dwell in a small Utopia. We had no bread-and-butter worries. We lived hardily, in temperatures that appalled the American Rhodes Scholars, taking our cold baths in colder bedrooms and flat tin pans, but with coal fires, flaming or incandescent, to give us all the ancient comfort of the 'hearth'.

We divided our days between sharpening our wits,

exercising our bodies and talking to friends chosen by
ourselves. We were under a gentle discipline, far less
restrictive than the social and economic pressures of the
world beyond the College walls ; but nobody inter-
fered with our freedom of thought and expression. We
were mildly and rather self-consciously unconventional
(but since we belonged to a race which spends much of
its leisure in making and observing rules — for games,
or sports, or clubs, or social intercourse — our uncon-
ventionality did not blossom into anything to speak of).
We had no slogans. We admired and envied originality.
Our society was not classless, because birds of a feather,
if uncaged, will always flock together. But 'class', with
us, was a matter of affinity, and had nothing to do with
who our fathers were or how much money they had.
Surplus money, indeed, for the few that possessed it,
was used for entertaining friends, but could never buy
social success, whereas social failure, nine times out of
ten, was your own fault. We lived under men we
could, and did, look up to, and all our loyalties were
spontaneous ; we had no colonels, party chiefs, or
'bosses', towards whom our natural feelings had to be
subdued by duty. As for power, we never even thought
about it : a sure mark of Utopia.

There was in my day a pleasant custom, which I
hope persists, whereby Balliol men who had lately, or
not so lately, 'gone down' returned again and again,
for a week-end or a night, to keep in touch with the
next generation. Number XIV staircase was a recognised port of call for these friendly seniors, on their way
to 'Sligger's' rooms, and through my luck in living not
only on that staircase, but in a ground-floor set, I came,
in time, to be accepted as a link in a chain of Balliol men

that stretched, at both ends, well beyond the limits of
my own four years at Oxford. Indeed, it is difficult for
me to remember that I was never 'up' with Aubrey
Herbert, or Bron Lucas, or 'Beb' Asquith, or 'Bongie'
(Sir Maurice Bonham-Carter), or Anthony and Francis
Henley, the two 'Bear' Warres, 'Nibs' Nisbet, John
Kennaway, Charlie Meade, Charles Ponsonby and
many others, so firmly founded were these friendships
upon the Balliol rock from which we were all hewn.
A most vivid picture of my freshman days is the sudden
appearance in my rooms, one winter's night, of a new
face, framed in the upturned collar of a fur coat, the
most beautiful, subtle and distinguished young man's
countenance that I had ever set eyes upon. The face
was Raymond Asquith's. I was never of the calibre to
enter into the inner courts of Raymond's intimacy, for
which high and fastidious scholarship was needed, but
as a young man beginning at the Bar I had much kindness from him, and knew him well enough to savour,
when we lunched together at the Union Club, the taste
of his wit and charm and penetrating intelligence. I
am not one of those who believe that had Raymond
survived the first Great War, he would have followed
in his father's footsteps and attained celebrity in public
life. He was without ambition as well as physically
delicate ; and, although nothing could have prevented
him reaching the heights of his profession had he cared
to climb them, I doubt if he would have cared. What
he prized was leisure — leisure to read and re-read the
classic authors, and to cultivate friendships, and to
pierce with wit and irony the shams and hypocrisies of
our civilisation. The country lost in Raymond, not a
leader, but a unique human being, astringent, pro-

vocative and leavening in intercourse, warm and loyal at core. His youthful arrows had struck at those who chanced, in crossing his morning path, to offend his fastidiousness ; his mature ones, had he lived, might well have destroyed more prominent offenders. When the springs of thought and of writing were polluted, between the wars, by some tributary 'streams of consciousness', Raymond's cool and classic taste might well have served — who knows ? — to shame their muddied sources. He would, I think, have been a stern and authoritative guardian of good things.

His friend and contemporary, Aubrey Herbert, was cast in a very different mould. With a small, close-cropped bullet head, myopic eyes, a slight unathletic figure, groping uncertain hands, a faintly wizened face, and untidy, inappropriate clothes, Aubrey gave no hint, to one seeing him for the first time, of his extraordinary physical capacities. Short-sighted almost to blindness, he was a tough and dare-devil scaler of walls and precipices. There are some tall houses in King Edward Street, at Oxford, at which I still look up with a trembling at the knees when I remember how Aubrey traversed the face of them, forty feet up, with finger-holds alone and a swing from ledge to ledge. But these bodily feats were by-play. Aubrey 'lived in high romance'. Every girl was a poem to him, and to most of them he wrote one. He simmered and bubbled and boiled over with enthusiasm. It might be Garibaldi, or Turkish baths, or a liqueur called Tangerino, or his brigand-friends in Albania, or the bloody Bismarck — (his hates were as ardent as his loves) — for whatever Aubrey had in his head he made at least a phrase, sometimes an epigram, often some verses. He delighted in

words as some women in jewels, but he did not keep
them, as most jewels are kept, for great occasions.
Aubrey soaking in his unbelievably hot bath at Pixton
after shooting would be as lavish with his phrases, to
myself waiting my turn in a bath-towel, as to his
favourite girl at a dinner-party. All his thoughts were
open and at our service ; he had no reserves with those
he liked ; and because his mind was singularly original
and fertile, as well as romantic, there was no resisting
the charm of his conversation. His activities were
abreast of his knightly imagination. He became the
confidant of Young Turks and the hero of Albanian
chieftains. One of these, whose life Aubrey had saved
in some vendetta, insisted on becoming his benefactor's
body-servant — 'great man though I am in my own
country'. He stood behind Aubrey, at pheasant shoots,
in kilt and embroidered jacket, and disconcerted even
his master by cutting off the heads of fallen birds with
the scimitar-like weapon he carried in his belt. I
remember a letter he wrote from Albania, full of longing for Pixton. 'There was a girl called Anne that
worked in your kitchen. She had eyes like a gazelle.
Salute her — she loved me very much.'

Aubrey had the rare gift of picking up foreign
languages, and even dialects, in a matter of weeks. But
he did not travel only for fun and adventure. With
his friend George Lloyd he made himself an expert in
Near Eastern affairs, drawing his knowledge of the
peoples concerned from their responsiveness to his
imaginative sympathy, and from their appreciation of
his high-bred gallantry. When he spoke on his own
subjects in the House of Commons, he was listened to
as much for his authoritative knowledge as for his gift

D

of words.   But for all his fascinating and endearing
natural endowments, he would have said, with Belloc :
'Balliol made me'.

I owed my friendship with Aubrey to his younger
brother Mervyn, who had already taken a First in
History when I went up to Balliol, but stayed on in the
hopes of a Cricket Blue and an All Souls' Fellowship.
He achieved neither, but failure never damped his
eager, demonstrative high spirits.   Mervyn's devotion
to his chosen friends was uncritical almost to embarrassment.   Why he chose me almost at sight, a wet-bob
freshman, I have never understood, for his antipathies
were legion, but choose me he did, and endless fun we
had together.   With a strain of high seriousness, nour-
ished by his friend and tutor 'Fluffy' Davis, where
work was concerned, on Saturday nights Mervyn could
be rollicking.

His enthusiasms sometimes miscarried.   In the long
vacations he played cricket for Somerset, and when
Somerset played Oxford in the Parks, Mervyn gave a
dinner for a very famous cricketer indeed.   A fair-
haired giant was received by Mervyn at the Randolph
Hotel as if he had been the Prince of Wales.   We were
led up in turn to shake hands with the illustrious guest,
who beamed upon us graciously.   We sat down to
dinner in a private room, a party of twenty at least.
The great man waved away the champagne and asked
for whisky.   A square-faced bottle was placed before
him.   He did his own replenishing.   Towards the end
of dinner he rose, swaying but resolved, to make a
speech.   It was quite a long speech.   We had all drunk
plenty of champagne ;   we were not maiden ladies ;
we were in the mood of tolerant indulgence induced

by a good dinner. But I shall never forget the devastating effect of that cricketer's speech upon the company, or the consternation in Mervyn's eyes. The
speaker, fortunately, was unaware of his own impact
upon us, for in sitting down he quietly passed out. I
was one of those enlisted to carry his enormous inert
body to a cab, and to put it into a bed in Mervyn's
digs in Teddy Street. Next day the celebrated player
was as brilliant as ever in the Parks, but Mervyn was
making the round of his guests, apologising. For one
who loved his friends as he did, to have to listen to
those whisky-born assumptions about their tastes and
habits had been agonising.

Mervyn was happiest when entertaining his friends
at Pixton where he and Aubrey lived with their
widowed mother, Lady Carnarvon, and his half-sister,
Lady Vera. Pixton stands on a hill in a rolling wooded
park near Dulverton in Somerset, in the midst of sharp
valleys and hanging covers. I travelled thither with
Mervyn for the first time at the end of a winter term,
and after changing at Taunton we rode in the cab of the
engine. The glow from the smoke-stack was reflected
from above by tree-trunks climbing high banks, and
from below by sudden patches of water. Sparks
streamed continuously over our heads ; the night was
frosty and star-lit. I thought it a romantic way to
travel, but Mervyn was talking County cricket with
the fireman. The shooting-party consisted of eleven
guns, all Balliol men. Mervyn was passing through a
phase of hostility towards young women, whom he
regarded as spoil-sports, and only one girl had been
invited to meet the eleven men. She had been asked
in order to ensure Raymond Asquith's presence, for he

was then triumphantly courting Miss Katharine Horner.
So this lovely tall creature, large-eyed, long-lashed,
with a magnolia complexion, moved silently among us,
with words only for Raymond, but doing no service
to Mervyn's party-line.   And we should have been
even more reluctant to agree with our host that stag-
parties were the best, had he not expressly excepted
from his misogyny his half-sister, Lady Vera.

Fred Gosse, the head-keeper at Pixton, was also
Harbourer to the staghounds, and so a public character
known throughout Devon and Somerset.   But he
seemed to like his eleven Balliol guns and became part
of the day's fun in a way few head-keepers do.   The
days were strenuous.   When the far-off beats were to
be driven, we breakfasted before sunrise, and when
Fred said 'Up over, Gentlemen !' it was 'up' indeed.
The winter woods hung from the narrow ridges like
rugs thrown over a rail.   Bron Lucas fitted an iron-claw
to his wooden leg, out of respect to those steep pitches.
The pheasants were not many, but flew as only wild
birds will.   Fred's cheerful red face beamed as kindly
on those of us who mostly missed as on those, like Bron
and Mervyn, who mostly hit.   We were all of us out
for fun, which is not, in England, the invariable companion of sport.   Trudging home one evening along a
valley bottom, where the ruts were already crisp with
frost, I found myself walking with Edmond Warre.   A
full moon had just risen and stood for a moment, gold
just touching black, on the naked brow of a dark hill.
As we watched it, a great Exmoor stag walked into the
enormous yellow circle, and paused, with antlers held
high, as if conscious of his own lordly silhouette.   It
was a chance in a million.   That was fifty years ago,

and we talk of it still. Later on, at midnight, muffled and great-coated, the Balliol eleven sat on the Pixton lawn, the moon now small and silver and sailing high and the hoar-frost white on grass and twig, and drank hot mulled claret, heavily spiced. 'Bear' Warre was a friend of Hilaire Belloc, and it was little wonder that we burst into song outside the quiet, shuttered house. A cock-pheasant protested, crowing from the wood that fell away below us. I had probably missed him earlier on, but I could not care.

A party that contained Bron Lucas, Aubrey Herbert, Raymond and Herbert Asquith and the precociously wise and witty Alec Cadogan, did not talk and laugh in merely undergraduate fashion. These older men had their links with the world, and for all Mervyn's delight in high jinks, he was already becoming absorbed in his ambitions for a career in diplomacy. And so, apart from the fun and the friendships, I must count my many happy visits to Pixton as a part of my Balliol education. I heard talk there of public men and world affairs ; a very great deal about poetry, which ran continually in the heads of Aubrey and his sister, and not a little about history, for the whole Herbert family sat at the feet of 'Fluffy' Davis. Their father had twice been Colonial Secretary, as well as Lord-Lieutenant of Ireland and a classical scholar, and the 'ruling class' tradition that shaped their outlook was one of responsibility and high behaviour, modestly concealed by gaiety and humour. Pixton was a good house for a young man to frequent.

If I was in any danger of thinking, after the kindness and tolerance I met with at that first Pixton party, that I could slip easily and on my own merits into the good graces of the older generation, I was soon saved from any such mistake. On returning through a heavy thunderstorm to my own rooms one morning in my first year, I found seated in the window-seat an enormous man, wearing a check cap and cape and smoking a pipe. He had a great head, a heavy black moustache, a high colour and thick dark eyebrows that lifted for a second as he looked me up and down. He did not speak, but turned away to puff at his pipe and to watch the downpour. His formidable aspect, and his silence, made me nervous. Besides, they were my rooms and I was the host ; luncheon was set out upon the table ; he looked massively settled and at home. I felt it to be up to me to say something. The thunder crashed and the rain fell in sheets, offering an obvious topic. 'Heavy storm,' I said. The big man turned and stared at me, ruminating. Then he slowly removed his pipe from his mouth. 'Is that a good remark ?' he asked. Fortunately Archie Gordon, who had invited Arnold Ward to lunch, came in at that moment and introduced me. But it was a long time before Arnold, who in those days used his great abilities in manufacturing 'good remarks' with the same single-mindedness with which he later wasted them in playing bridge, regarded me as worthy of his notice. And on my side I was not only paralysed in his company, but thought him a boor, which he was not. In later years I found in him much entertainment — he had a fabulous gift of declaiming extempore verse on any topic supplied to him — and he for his part accepted me readily as a worthy member of his audience.

Then there was Reginald Farrer, to remind me from time to time of my own mediocrity. He was to become celebrated as traveller, discoverer and collector of rare plants from China and the Himalayas, and authoritative as well as delightful writer on gardens and gardening. His pygmy body — which I once heard described in his presence by the late Lord Oxford, in a moment of inexplicable aberration when playing a parlour-game, as 'the soul's dark cottage, battered and decayed' — was inhabited by a spirit of extraordinary courage and resolution. A fascinating and often brilliant talker, he had to overcome the handicaps of having no roof to his mouth, and of a voice both high and harsh. He was often mistaken for a Japanese. He allowed none of these disadvantages, which I have set so plainly down, to disconcert him. He went as hardily, even jauntily, into all social gatherings as into the toils and privations of untrodden Asia. I had much kindness from him, including hospitality in his home at Ingleborough, high in the Yorkshire fells ; but he never allowed me to forget my place. He had a peculiar way of snorting — literally and loudly — to express contempt, and if ever my voice was heard at a table where Reginald sat, it ceased upon a snort. I have sometimes wondered why he felt that one so dim beside his own refulgence needed this continuous discipline. It may be that he half-guessed, and resented, that the normal man's reaction to his physical abnormalities was to feel chivalrous. Chivalry, he may well have felt, was for him, not for me, to exhibit ; and it may be that if I could have attacked him freely, I should have been less snorted at. It must be maddening for the better man to find himself tenderly handled by the worse. I was too inexperienced to understand this ; one must be mature to recognise that pity is a wrong done to one too proud, or too courageous, to pity himself. At any rate, I prefer this explanation to the more simple one that my conversation was invariably foolish.

In later life, what I had endured from Arnold Ward's silences and Reginald's snorts stood me in good stead, for the experience had toughened me for an even harder ordeal : that of lunching with yet another of my Balliol seniors, Oswald Falk ('Foxy'), who, in the intimacy of a *tête-à-tête*, would frequently say nothing at all in reply to some of my observations. There are few things more disconcerting than to be face to face with a fabulously intelligent man and to get no other acknowledgement of your remarks than a blank stare. I would wait hopefully — could it be that he was thinking over what I had said ? But no. After a prolonged silence he would broach another subject. He was kindly and friendly, but ignorance or superficiality struck him dumb. Thanks to my early training, I was always more than willing for further encounters.

Reminiscences of the College days of men of mark can be fascinating, and had there been no first Great War to devour my generation, I might well, today, have been sure of attention for my memories of more than one distinguished statesman and more certainly of one Field-Marshal hardly less renowned as poet. As it is, although the name of Julian Grenfell will survive in Anthologies, and that of Charles Lister quicken, here and there, the dead leaves of a few contemporary social memoirs, a name like John Douglas Radcliffe can mean no more upon a page than if noticed, in passing, carved upon a village headstone. Yet had he not fallen at Hooge in 1915, how pressingly today might I, his closest friend both at Eton and Balliol, have been invited to print my recollections of his formative years !

How entertaining it would have been to learn that this
massive elder statesman, whose determination to learn
by experience had convinced his countrymen that
political constancy may be a fault, not a merit, had been
no less steadfastly changeable in his callow youth ! But
the young Fellow of All Souls died, a good reluctant
soldier, in battle ; and few will care to hear of how a
somewhat sluggish Eton caterpillar was turned, not by
Nature but himself, into the strong-winged, strong-
willed butterfly of our hopes. So I must leave him,
who had in the highest degree I ever met with the
humility and wisdom to profit by experience without
the smallest surrender of integrity. To be interesting,
it is necessary to survive.

Julian Grenfell has survived, as the author of one of
the loveliest of all poems. (I must in candour say that,
when reading it to myself, I omit the stanza about the
horses who

—show him nobler powers,
O patient eyes, courageous hearts !

because as a private in the Inns of Court Squadron, and
later a Yeoman, I got to know horses very well indeed,
and am convinced that they are neither brave nor
patient, although they can be placid enough when
entirely comfortable. But then so can we all.) He
was two years my junior at Balliol, but had rooms, as
a freshman, just above mine on Number XIV staircase,
and I came to know him well. Our nickname for him
in those days was 'the Rough Man', or 'Roughers', and
he took it as a sincere compliment. He was at that time
a body-worshipper. His main cares were his own body
and that of his black greyhound, Slogbottom (about
whom he also wrote a fine poem). When stripped for

boxing, Julian's body could not be faulted, and he
kept it, by hard all-round use, as lithe and sinewy as
Slogbottom's. With a gentle, and in some ways a very
humble disposition, he liked to pose as a Milo, and
would drive Philip Sassoon, of whose Oriental and
cushioned 'digs' he disapproved, out of College with
an Australian stock-whip, cracking the prodigious lash
within inches of Sassoon's sleek head. This performance
had a curious sequel. During the battle of Loos, a
few weeks after Julian's death from wounds, my
Yeomanry Regiment stood saddled up, night and day,
in the grounds of General Rawlinson's château, ready
to gallop through the 'gap' which our optimistic
leaders still believed could be opened by the infantry
through that immense tangle of pit-heads, slag-heaps,
canals, trenches and barbed wire. After a sleepless
night spent attempting to get some shelter under juniper
bushes from the incessant rain, we were gazing, chilled
and red-eyed, at the noble entrance of the château from
which we expected our orders to come forth, when a
very slim, very dapper young officer, with red tabs on
his collar and shining boots, began to descend the steps.
It was Philip Sassoon, 'Rawly's' A.D.C. I have never
been one of those who think that Staff Officers are
unduly coddled, or that they should share the discomforts of the troops. Far from it. But there are moments
when the most entirely proper inequality, suddenly
exhibited, can be riling. Tommy Lascelles, not yet
His or Her Majesty's Private Secretary, but a very
damp young lieutenant who had not breakfasted, felt
that this was one of those moments. Concealed by a
juniper bush, he called out 'Pheeleep ! Pheeleep ! I
see you !' in a perfect mimicry of Julian's warning cry

from his window when he had spied Sassoon, who
belonged to another College, treading delicately through
Balliol Quad. The beauteous A.D.C. stopped, lifted
his head like a hind snuffing the wind, then turned and
went rapidly up the steps and into the doorway. Did
he think it was Julian's voice from the grave ? Or had
he merely remembered some more pressing errand for
his General ? We shall never know. But the incident
cheered up the dripping Yeomen. There is irony in
the thought of how much, had Julian lived, he would
have found to like and admire in the sagacious and
gifted Minister of the Crown into which the young
A.D.C. eventually blossomed. Both had a passion for
beauty, as well as for getting things done.

For all his animal high spirits, Julian as an undergraduate was not at peace with himself. For one thing,
he was at odds with his home. There was something
simple and primitive in him that was outraged by the
perfection of well-bred luxury at Taplow. He was
depressed by 'rows with Mother', waged by correspondence, in which Julian was the attacker. It must
have been hard for Lady Desborough to have her
expertise in hostess-ship roughly handled by a nineteen-
year-old son, who was her pride. He, on his side, felt
that there was something artificial and unreal in her
deft manipulation of a procession of week-end parties,
lightly skimming the cream from the surface of life.
What he wanted of her he could never explain ; you
cannot expect an exquisite woman of the world to wear
sweaters and follow greyhounds on foot. But Julian
had a passion for red-blooded down-to-earthiness, for
action and adventure, and, with youthful intolerance,
fiercely resented the easy, cushioned existence of

Edwardian society. So he attacked and, to judge from his rather rueful midnight confidings, usually got the worst of it. Had he been able to guess, in those halcyon days, at the greatness and gallantry of his mother's heart, to be tested, in so few years, by the death of all three sons, things would have been different. As it was, he fretted and rebelled.

Moody, affectionate, romantic as he was, Julian was above all made for combat. There was never any question in our minds but that he would become a distinguished soldier and leader of men. What I myself did not then foresee was 'Into Battle'. Yet, when it appeared, to place him for ever among the English Poets, I remember no feeling of surprise. Rather did I feel : 'Only Julian could have written that !' Such immediate unastonished recognition of a friend wearing a halo must mean that, subconsciously, one had known all along that it would suit him.

A legend has somehow grown up, that Julian was one of a little band of Balliol brothers as knightly as they were brilliant, who might, had they survived, have flavoured society with an essence shared by them all. Of two of these, Billy Grenfell and John Manners, I can say nothing, as they did not come up to Balliol until I had gone down. But the others— Charles Lister, Patrick Shaw-Stewart and Edward Horner — were, though junior, contemporaries and friends of my own. As far as these three and Julian are concerned, the legend is very wide of the mark. Apart from their delight in each other's company, and their common gallantry in the exacting tests of war, few men could have been less alike in temperament, character and outlook.

Charles Lister, although he liked to hunt and shoot,

was a creature all mind and heart. His body, unlike
Julian's, was rarely a pleasure to him. His long white
patrician face, crowned with a tight-curling lack-lustre
mat, that could not be smoothed or parted, was often
greenish, for his inside could never be relied upon. He
was frequently sick. He was inept at all ball-games.
He was ungainly in his movements, with a nervous
habit of twisting about his arms and legs and fingers,
and of tying himself into knots, when arguing or holding forth or being funny. His laugh was unearthly,
and almost continuous, for nobody could be so amusing
or so easily amused. He was at once the most serious
and the most frivolous of us all. When sent down in
the middle of the term for waltzing round a bonfire
with the Junior Dean of Trinity, he went straight off
to work at an East End Mission. He had compassion,
and a sense of responsibility to the under-privileged, to
a degree unknown to the rest of us, complacent and
self-centred in our busy preoccupations. It was these
sensibilities that led him when still an Eton boy to join
the Labour Party — the cloth-capped, Keir Hardie-led,
class-ridden party of the nineteen-hundreds — and to
manage to combine, at Oxford, a First in Greats with
sudden raids into anti-sweating, Fabianism and strikes.
He carried himself with unselfconscious gaiety in all
he did. His good humour was invincible ; his conversation, however fantastic or flippant, was salted with
thought. As a human being Charles was in a class by
himself in our generation, and although he had begun
a career in the Diplomatic Service when war broke out,
we never doubted that he would, in due course, be
driven by his fiery and undaunted daemon into public
life. Into what party, it is impossible to say. He had

already broken with doctrinaire Socialism. With the
fervour of a young Gladstone, the imagination of a
young Dizzy, and a selflessness that neither possessed,
Charles must have qualified from the first as statesman,
not politician ; but all one can say about his platform
is that it is hard to imagine any man or woman, after
hearing and seeing Charles Lister, voting against him.
When his name is so often coupled with that of Julian,
it should not be overlooked that, had both lived to
fame and performance, Julian would have taken, and
gladly, his orders from Charles.

When Charles was sent down for dancing with a
Dean, it was Patrick Shaw-Stewart who found the
appropriate epitaph : 'I wist not, brethren, that he was
high priest', to engrave upon the incised headstone that
flanked the entrance to Number XIV staircase. For
in fact the Dean of Trinity had been of so slight
and youthful an appearance that Charles had every
excuse, after a bump-supper, for pressing him into a
reluctant waltz. And it was Patrick who, draped in a
bath-towel and holding a scroll, pronounced Charles'
funeral oration in the Quad at the moment when the
Master's lecture was debouching from Hall.

He was a wit, and a distinguished scholar, holding
his own even with Ronnie Knox, winning the New-
castle at Eton and, at Oxford, the Ireland, Craven
and Hertford Scholarships, with Firsts in Mods and
Greats. He was elected a Fellow of All Souls. He
was the close and loyal friend of both Julian and Charles.
He was straightforward and reliable, affectionate and
tolerant. For the sheer taste of good company, I would
have rather dined *tête-à-tête* with Patrick at the Grid
than with any man of my day. For all that I am sure

that, seen through God's microscope, he was, at that time, a creature of a lower order than were those two friends. For while they were both, in their respective fashions, made restless and tormented by the injustices or superficialities of society, Patrick had no misgivings about Mammon. One might liken him to a red-headed, Scottish, temperate, upper-class F. E. Smith, with whom he shared the brilliance, the loyalty to friends, and the determination to win the glittering prizes of wealth, luxury and social distinction. His first ambition was to make money. With gifts that would have brought him to the top of the legal or any other profession, he chose to go into the City. At twenty-five he was a managing-director of Baring Brothers. After making a fortune he would undoubtedly have aimed at, and achieved, the Treasury Bench and eventually a peerage, which he would have enjoyed. All the more must his metamorphosis when war broke out, seen through that same celestial microscope, have delighted the Observer. For whereas Julian went to war with high zest, thirsting for combat, and Charles with his habitual selfless dedication to a cause, Patrick had all to lose. We are not, perhaps, always sufficiently appreci-ative of the materialist who goes cheerfully into mortal danger. Unless he be a Muslim, he can hardly hope to find in death, come what may, the good food and wine, the social consequence, the sensuous satisfactions, the screened and sheltered ease, to be achieved through wealth and prominence in Edwardian society. Patrick wanted all these things ; but, knowing the risks, let go his hold of them and went cheerfully to war. He, of the three, made the most costly sacrifice.

Edward Horner, so strangely associated in legend

with these three diverse yet, each in his way, remarkable young men, was a social butterfly, fluttering unashamed. For all his pre-Raphaelite good looks, and much charm, it was as impossible not to be recurrently angry with him as to be angry with him for long. He came back, after each scolding, with the affectionate eyes and caressing ways of a faithful dog who has been beaten. He had great physical courage, displayed at Oxford by riding, an indifferent horseman, in 'Grinds' in which he well knew he would fall off, and pre-eminently in the war, to which he insisted on returning after recovering from wounds. He had no ambition except to sip honey. Nobody would have laughed more heartily than Edward at the idea that he would some day be canonised in the same batch as Charles Lister and Julian Grenfell. All the same, the world would be poorer without butterflies, and a brave butterfly must be remembered with affection and respect.

I have met young people of today to whom these four names, even after a second World War, are familiar, but I cannot expect to arouse interest in others no less cherished in the memories of the few survivors of my generation. Victor Barrington-Kennett, George Fletcher, Bob Brandt, Mervyn Higgins, Ted Shuttleworth must, like Douglas Radcliffe, be left in private keeping. All men of promise, vivid and vital, they salted our little society, and made the Quad a place of daily enlivening encounters. The first war took them all. Jasper Ridley survived it, to make his mark in many ways. He was notable, as an undergraduate, for the contrast between the solid gravity of his outward appearance and the skipping, frolicking spirit imprisoned in that elder-statesmanlike form. He looked a sage even as a schoolboy, and in many ways he was a sage, but his sagacity was laced with dancing humour, and his strong good sense with refreshing nonsense. He had early ambitions to shine at the Union, but being, like Plutarch's Phæax, 'the best of talkers, and of speakers worst' soon had the sense, as always, not to cry for the moon. He was busy at the political clubs ; having on one occasion promised, and forgotten, to write a paper for the Chatham or the Canning, he asked me, at the eleventh hour, to write one for him. I knew his mind, and could write 'New thoughts for old Tories' at a sitting ; but he was taken aback when, having been invited, as a reward, to hear him read it, I rose, when it was my turn to speak, and tore it to shreds. He said it was treachery, but was appeased when I argued that it was his, not my, paper that I had been called upon to write. The Dons regarded him, rightly, as a main pillar of the College, and had a severe shock when 'Fluffy' Davis arraigned him, already a graduate, before a College meeting for 'rioting' in the Quad. The lamps had been broken, and the Quad was in darkness when Davis, searching for culprits, found a figure attempting to look like part of an elm-bole. 'But what makes you think it was — er — Mr. Ridley ?' asked the Master.

'Because when I told him who I was, he said, "My God !" and ran away.'

Jasper was acquitted, by judges determined to acquit, without being called upon for his defence. Fortunately, for he could not tell a lie.

Jasper's nickname was at one time 'How-much-the-greatest-and-how-much-the-best', given affectionately, not ironically, and if it did not stick to him through

E

life, that was only because, like the names of Cromwell's Ironsides, it was on the long side. If, in after years, he became more of a sage through responsibilities and the burden of almost unexampled private griefs, yet the light-footed imp within him never died. He became, rather to our surprise, a devotee, patron and administrator of modern painting, besides one of Nature's Trustees.

His first cousin, Archie Gordon — a year my senior on Number XIV — was the most irrepressibly high-spirited young man I have ever known. He was tall and strong, and a little rugged, and through his round, comely face there shone the light of his eager enjoyment. Idealistic, with a streak of Scottish puritanism, he was a natural disciple, always looking for a Master at whose feet to sit, and whose sayings to cherish and to repeat. A print of Mr. Gladstone hung in his rooms, and he was the first man of my own age I had met, except Hugh O'Neill at Eton, to be preoccupied with current politics. His eager Cabinet-making during the landslide of 1906 was my first taste of political discussion on the personal side, with Alec Cadogan playing Taper to Archie's Tadpole, and when, in the new triumphant Liberal Government, Archie's father, Lord Aberdeen, went to Ireland as Lord-Lieutenant, and Archie to London to be fitted with the gorgeous uniform of a Dublin Castle A.D.C., his bubble and glee were unbounded.

Archie did not take to me at once. He could not approve of a freshman getting a Blue in his second term, for, like Mervyn Herbert, he did not share the indifference to such things prevalent in the College at large. (His own half-Blue for golf gave him much satisfaction.) But his natural friendliness was immense, and he liked being liked, and since I fell from the first under the spell of his gaiety and charm, his initial reserve was not of long duration. Archie was a perfectionist, always struggling, with good but not quite tip-top abilities, to find the right expression, the finest model, the most reliable touchstone. In spite of his ebullience, he was humble and a hero-worshipper, intent on self-education.

There was a streak of recklessness in Archie. I shall never forget a moment of agony when, at a week-end party at Hatfield, Archie bet somebody half a crown that he could loft a golf-ball with a mashie off the hard gravel in the forecourt clean over one of the wings of that historic house; the bet was taken; Archie half topped his shot; the ball went sailing straight towards the stained-glass window of the Chapel. It hit an upright mullion and bounced back harmlessly, but for a small chip on the stone. Had it gone through the window, what conceivable excuse could Archie have made to his host? But he only grinned, and forked out half a crown.

At an after-dinner game of 'Epigrams', Archie once described himself as 'a wave breaking in sunshine'. It was extraordinarily apt. He had all the impetus, the gathered strength of a breaker, spending itself in the sun-lit foam of laughter and good humour. He was mortally injured in a motor-smash before the first Great War, but had he lived, there can be little doubt that the strength of that wave, drawn up from a profundity of character and conscience, would have supported, in years to come, a full share of the country's burdens in war or in peace. Sturdy, Scottish high-mindedness, aerated with the bubbles of enthusiasm, could have never been amiss in the troubled years to come.

Is it too late now, after a second Great War and the loss in battle of yet another generation, to write as I have written about some who were, after all, only a handful of young men of promise, to be matched many times over not only in other Colleges than Balliol, and in Universities other than Oxford, but wherever young men were then coming to their full strength and capacities ? I do not think so. For whenever I read the gossiping kinds of writer, like Plutarch or Pepys or Creevy, who tell about persons of no importance, I find a particular pleasure in having the names of those persons recorded and their appearances described. To recall the past vividly, there must be displayed in it not types but individuals, as busy with their private, fugitive concerns as we are with our own. So that, even in the least pretentious of records, it makes for easy reading if names are given and pictures drawn. They were very solid in their day, those figures crossing and re-crossing the Quad : Alec Cadogan with hair beautifully brushed, and the air even then of a Permanent Secretary for Foreign Affairs, in neat tweeds, eschewing the grey flannel trousers of the rest of us ; Archie Gordon in a huge cloth cap, worn a little askew, and a rough shooting-jacket, rubbing 'Sligger's' offended curly head ; Jasper Ridley looking like a Prime Minister and behaving like an April lamb ; Julian Grenfell, ruddy as the boy David, in shorts and a ribbed sweater ; Patrick Shaw-Stewart displaying a vast area of red gum as he grinned at a joke of Charles Lister's ; Charles twining his awkward limbs like tendrils round a bench while making the joke ; Victor

Barrington-Kennett with the face of an arch-, and Edward Horner with that of a fallen, angel; Douglas Radcliffe, massive and shy, trying, and failing, to hide his inward fires behind a smoke-screen of cynicism. They came and went, casual or purposeful, beneath the trees that stand there still; they were solid, as I have said, and eager and busy and red-blooded, and if only because they were once a living part of a great College and a great country, they have a claim to be remembered.

III

I WENT up to Oxford in the year which was marked by the arrival of the first batch of Rhodes Scholars. These rather elderly young men had been chosen, in America and Germany as well as in all parts of the Empire, for 'character' and athletic prowess as much as for scholarship. It was rumoured that they had come to teach as much as to learn. If this were so, those we were lucky enough to have at Balliol were entirely successful in disguising their mission. Paterson and Rose and Jim Macdonnel from Canada, de Witt Hutchings from the U.S.A., Percy Lewis from South Africa, were all gentle, modest men who, mature as they were among the other freshmen, made no overt attempt to invigorate us with clean winds from the great open spaces. They appeared, rather, to be even more sensible than ourselves to the enchantments of Oxford, and, on the physical side, to be impressed, tough athletes as they were, by the hardiness of a race who could sleep in unheated bedrooms and keep clean without hot baths. There was, not unnaturally, some mutual eye-opening to be got through. De Witt Hutchings, great Princeton footballer and member of the 'Ideal' baseball team, was clearly asking for our sympathy when he described how a rival University — could it have been Yale ? — arrived to play Princeton at football with a negro in their team. 'Can you beat it ?'

'Was he good ?' we asked.

'We never found out. When the whistle blew, we just left the ball alone and broke every bone in his body.' He was genuinely astonished at our shocked disapproval. Yet 'Hutch' was the kindest and gentlest of men, who, after going down, spent years in studying the Italian primitives.

Two stories of these first Rhodes Scholars came from Merton. One of the new arrivals there was a Professor of Latin in some small Southern University. The College statutes demanded some sort of preliminary examination from all new entrants, but the Fellows of Merton felt that they could hardly ask a Professor of Latin to share the elementary papers set to boys fresh from the Upper Fifth Form. So, just for good order's sake, they asked him to turn a short poem by Browning into some Catullan metre. He sat for a time poring over the Browning, then rose and went to the monitoring Don.

'I guess I better put you wise right now. I don't know any Latin.'

'But — but we were told you were Professor of Latin !'

'Why, that's so, but I got my Professorship for puoily po-litical reasons.'

The other Merton Rhodes Scholar was a full-blooded negro. I remember him well — enormous, woolly-headed, black as ebony, rolling the whites of his eyes. He was courteously received by the Warden, Mr. George Brodrick. They had a pleasant conversation, and Mr. Brodrick wished him success and shook hands.

The huge black man went to the door. He hesitated —
something seemed to be on his mind. He turned, and
came resolutely back to the Warden's table.

'Mr. Warden, there's just one more thing I feel I
ought to tell you.'

'Well, Mr. Washington ?'

'It's just that — that I'm a gentleman of colour.'

At the end of their first year A. L. Smith asked one
of the American Rhodes Scholars what had most struck
him about Oxford. The American pondered for a
moment, then replied : 'That there are nearly three
thousand men here who would rather lose a game than
win it by cheating'. Those were the days when an
American runner in the first Olympic Games, having
been disqualified for elbowing the British half-miler off
the track, was welcomed home with brass bands and
presented with a Silver Cup to mark his countrymen's
appreciation of his 'brainy' running, and when American wet-bobs expressed their astonishment that the
boats and oars of Henley crews were not kept under
lock and key, and guarded by the police. Things have
changed indeed since those days. And I am sure that
the change is not due to the fact that the Americans
can now win at all sports without cheating. It is a
change of heart : part of the same process that turned
that great people from isolationism to unexampled
generosity. It is now up to Oxford clergymen to give
up praying for rain when it is Cambridge's turn to bat,
and vice versa.

H. J. Rose, one of our Balliol Rhodes Scholars, was
already a graduate of McGill, and a prodigious classic.
It fell to me to give him his first lessons in rowing. He
was of elephantine build and Johnsonian clumsiness, and

the tub rocked dangerously as he swung, not backwards
and forwards, but from side to side. I ordered him
to 'easy', and tried to explain that his swing should
be up and down the line of the boat's keel. 'In other
words', he said — and then followed a rapid speech
in Greek. He was visibly shocked that an Exhibitioner
of Balliol, even a freshman, should have to ask him to
translate.

'I was merely observing', he said, 'that what you
are asking me to do is to implement the Aristortelian
ductrine of the mesotes or mean.'

I could only say 'Yes'. But he never succeeded in
implementing it.

This business of 'tubbing' freshmen and of teaching
them the elements of oarsmanship was infinitely tedious,
and has given me a wondering sympathy with school-
masters who spend their lives instructing Lower Forms.
Coaching a crew from the bank is interesting and
enjoyable ; the coach is an artist, a creator, and sees his
artifact grow under his hands ; but imparting the
grammar of rowing, with its endless repetitions, from
the stern of a gig, where the coach sits muffled, often
numb with cold, and hankering after exercise and enjoyment, was always, to me, a hateful duty. For four
years almost every hour that could be spared from
active rowing or the coaching of crews had to be spent
in this dismal manner. It is the wet-bob's burden, and
has to be borne ; but how often, as I walked down to
the Barge through Christ Church Meadows after a hard
morning's work, did I envy the happy dry-bobs off to
play football, or golf, or hockey, or to any form of
what I always thought of as 'fun'. I am not sure that
any kind of rowing, keen as are its excitements and

satisfactions, can be classed as 'fun', for which I have always had an unquenchable thirst.

But a rowing man at Oxford leads a life which may fairly be called 'dedicated'. It is curious to reflect upon the importance attached to a College's success upon the river by Master, Fellows and undergraduates alike. The pace at which a boat can be propelled by eight of the beefiest, but not by any means the most distinguished, young men in the College, would hardly seem, to a visitor from Mars, a matter of much concern to any but the crew. We — with the exception in my day of 'Fluffy' Davis — thought otherwise. We tubbed, and coached, and rowed for the honour and glory of Balliol. Personal distinction, the gaining of colours and renown, did not, as at Eton, come into it. Freshmen were systematically visited by senior oarsmen and urged to row, not because rowing is a fine manly sport, but as a public duty, a thing, exacting sacrifices, to be done for the good of the College. We used the Billy Graham approach. When a freshman from the North told me that, for recreation, he intended to 'do some cycling', I read him what was almost a religious homily. He had to be convinced of the shame and the sin of solitary rides about the Oxfordshire lanes when his College needed him in the second Togger. Not one, as far as I recollect, ever put the question of the visitor from Mars : 'How does the pace of a boat benefit a College ?' I should have been hard put to it for a reply, had the question been asked. But it never was. That a College was the better or worse for the rates at which its boats were propelled was axiomatic. If it was an illusion, it was one of those illusions, like many religious beliefs, for which we were ready to live laborious days and to practise not a little austerity. I have mentioned my own main sacrifice — that of fun. But training also has its minor hardships : early bed, no smoking, monotonous food, and the run in the Parks before breakfast on a winter's morning. And training was almost continuous for a successful oar ; College Fours in October followed by Trial Eights ; Torpids or, as in my own case, the University Eight in the Easter term ; and the College Eight in the Summer term, followed by Henley Regatta. The actual physical sensations of rowing in a good or even moderate Eight or Four are pleasurable ; and, as in all competitive sports, rowing has its thrills and its triumphs. But the servitude imposed by success is a heavy one ; and I doubt whether, but for this quasi-religious belief in the beneficent effect of fast boats upon the corporate welfare of the College, many of us could have been found willing to endure it for so long and so continuously. As it was we cheerfully dedicated ourselves, as I have said, to the service of an illusion which, by its almost universal acceptance, seemed to become a truth. If to go Head of the River, whether in Eights or Torpids, or merely to make bumps, can undeniably gladden the heart of a Strachan-Davidson or an A. L. Smith, then to go Head of the River, or to make bumps, becomes a thing of real moment.

When I went up as a freshman, the High Priest of this cult at Balliol was Archie Graham, the President of the O.U.B.C. Of slight build and almost girlish good looks, Archie was the toughest and most determined of oarsmen. He had an iron will and was, with charming manners, the complete martinet. Within a week I was rowing number three in the College Four behind Archie as stroke. It is a curious thing about rowing that, while a good crew should row as much like a machine as possible, nothing is done to enable the human bodies that propel the boat to work like machines. Were a mechanical eight to be constructed, in which eight robots of differing weights and various lengths of arm and leg were to row the boat, themselves being moved by some mechanical power, it is obvious that the length and leverage of each robot's oar would be different. Experiments in a tank would no doubt be made to ascertain the proper length of oar and outrigger, and the proper width of blade, to enable a six-foot robot weighing 14 stone to use his weight and reach to the best advantage, and so on throughout the boat. But in a human eight all members of the crew, whether they are short-armed men of 5 feet 4 inches weighing 10 stone, or long-armed men of 6 feet 4½ inches weighing 14 stone (like number three in that Balliol Four), are given oars of equal length and width of blade, and the 'leverage', which depends upon the length of the outrigger, is the same. Rowing men are so well accustomed to coping with this handicap, and to adapting their various shapes, sizes and weights to uniform tools, that for the most part they are unconscious of the resultant waste of effort, although they acknowledge the existence of the anomaly by occasionally shaving the blade of some lightweight oarsman rowing 'stroke'. But I shall never forget the humiliation of my debut, as an Eton eightsman of some reputation, in that Balliol Four. Rowing immediately behind a stroke nearly three stone lighter than myself, with a much shorter reach, but determined to maintain a high rate of stroking, I had to move my blade through about a couple of feet more water than he did, and yet finish cleanly at precisely the same moment as he. It was beyond my strength and skill. To Archie, as High Priest, my performance was not just incompetence, but sin. I was made to feel as an adulterer might feel, afloat in a small boat with the Archbishop of Canterbury. Luckily for me our coach was 'Rudy' Lehmann, once Editor of *Punch*. 'Rudy', whose compassion for under-dogs had made him a pro-Boer, for which act of courage he was for some years cold-shouldered by his fellow wet-bobs, took pity on the sinner. He let me feel that although a bad oar, I was not necessarily a bad man ; and dear 'Bill' Farrer, rowing at No. 2, also found ways of consoling me. He was Archie's close friend, and it may be that it was through his intercession that I obtained forgiveness, and eventually came to a firm and valued friendship with a very gallant man, who has carried himself, in undeserved adversity, with signal courage and steadfastness. And the time came when I, in turn, was High Priest, and in turn imputed sinfulness, as I have told, to a young heart set upon bicycling.

After Eton's broad river where, between races, we rowed and sculled for pleasure in summer weather, everything at Oxford seemed strange and different. Quite apart from the question of delinquency, it was winter, a season made for football, the river was narrow, unattractive and over-crowded ; 'Rudy' cheered us on when rowing a course with hunting noises, as if we were hounds, which made me want to laugh, an im-possible thing, physically, when you are rowing hard ; we raced out of sight of our opponents, the river being too narrow for boats to race abreast. When not rowing in the Four I was set to tubbing my fellow-freshmen, as I have described. Believing that my own career was finished, and not yet in possession of the Faith, I felt bored and disheartened. But no sooner was the racing over than I found one morning on my table a dirty little scrap of paper, left by Timms, the University Boatman, telling me to report that afternoon at the University Boathouse. I was to have another chance after all. In a Trial Eight, with other long-armed heavyweights, I felt more at home. We made lengthy voyages below locks in Nuneham Reach, where the autumn woods were golden ; the company was good, for I rowed behind Butts Howell, and as the Trial Eights took shape and got together, much of the old enjoyment, known only to wet-bobs, returned. By the day when our wet hair turned to icicles in Iffley Lock, and our fingers froze upon the oar, I was acclimatised, and recognised, without rebellion, that serious rowing, the kind that is done not for its own sake but for College and University, takes no account of weather or seasons. And on the College Barge, talking to the old hands, to Andrew Holden and Clinton Dawkins and such-like stalwarts of mediocre performance but unflagging loyalty, I was initiated into the cult, the mystique of the Balliol Boat Club, and unconsciously prepared, by their cheerful example, to become in due course a 'dedicated' man myself.

Before the Christmas vacation I was asked to 'come up' a few days before the Easter term, a favourable sign, and in the first fortnight of that term rowed alternately in the Varsity Eight and on a fixed seat in the Balliol Torpid. But an evening came when, in the Oxford Theatre, Timothy Simpson whispered to me that he had been eavesdropping, behind the *Pink'un*, at a conversation in Vincent's Club between Archie Graham and the Coach, the celebrated 'Flea', W. L. Fletcher. I might take it, said Timothy, that the crew was now settled, and that I was to row at No. 5. Never have I enjoyed a play more than I enjoyed it that night. Timothy's ill-gotten intelligence was correct. Even the early days of training for the Boat Race were full of glamour. The crew breakfasted and dined together in various College Halls and Common Rooms, often entertained by Dons who, like ourselves in the case of the College, had a mystical faith in the beneficent effect of our boat's speed upon the University at large. The standard breakfast consisted of Dover soles, of a size and plumpness not nowadays achieved by those delicious fish, followed by massive rump steaks, on each of which lay a poached egg. But had you been late at the rendezvous for the early run in the Parks by so much as a second, you breakfasted without butter. After dinner we drank a glass of port, and after my first glass of port I felt happy and comfortable and joined in the conversation, even, I believe, telling some amusing anecdotes. I did not, at the time, notice that Archie was not amused, nor did he himself say anything; but next day in the University Barge I was taken apart by the redoubtable 'Flea' himself and given a friendly warning. Freshmen, it seemed, who had not even received a Blue cannot, even fortified by port, be amusing. I was very much abashed, and ate my dinners in profound silence for some weeks. I was then chided by an old Blue, Archie Balfour, for being glum. I was learning behaviour. When, wearing our 'blues', we went to stay at the Leander Club at Henley I got a fright. For several nights I did not sleep a wink, and my weight fell by several ounces a day. Sir John Edwards-Moss, the Maecenas of Eton and Oxford wet-bobs, was called in. 'Does his bed lie north and south ?' he enquired. A compass was fetched : my bed lay east and west. 'How then can he sleep ?' said the experienced greybeard. The bed was shifted. I still did not sleep. The local doctor was sent for. He prescribed a sleeping-draught. 'That will knock you insensible for twelve hours,' he said. Not a wink of sleep did I get. The 'Flea' was disturbed. He sent me to Oxford by train to see Dr. Pigou-Symons, a clever Jew who 'vetted' many generations of Oxford oarsmen. Pigou examined me gravely. I had faced up to the end of my rowing career in the train ; all I hoped for now was to hear that, with care, I might yet live a few years. He told me that I was in rude health, and to go back and row harder and above all, 'no sleeping-draughts'. I returned to Henley, beaming from the train at the winter landscape so unexpectedly restored to me, and slept like a log.

One morning at Henley we took our early run in a thick fog. Visibility was about ten yards. In a narrow lane huge shapes loomed up before us. They were elephants, on their way to bathe in the river. It was a strange encounter.

In 1905 the Boat Race was still a National Institution. Every cab and bus driver in London tied a dark- or light-blue bow to his whip, every child wore a favour, and Frank Reynolds' ragged infant in a slum, back to the wall and half-throttled by the local Flashman, could still gasp out : 'No — not if you was to kill me I wouldn't be Cimebridge'.

So, on arrival at Putney, where we lived in a luxurious villa in Carlton Road, and where I had daily to remember, on passing 'No. 2 The Pines', that it was not for a freshman to expose his literary interests to his betters, we found ourselves public characters. School-boys crowded round with autograph books ; school-girls wrote little love-letters to Bill Farrer and Archie Graham, whose good looks fluttered them ; and the sporting papers had columns and columns every day about our weights, our rates of stroking and our faults. These were many, for we were only a second-class crew, but fortunately Cambridge were slower still, and in the race itself we led all the way and won by three lengths. So comfortable were we, after the first minute, that Archie Balfour at No. 4 found breath enough to shout, 'Swing, number five !' every few strokes throughout the race. I had the illusion that I was swinging all the time, and felt rather ungrateful, but the end was glory, and a champagne lunch, and a drive to the West End in a hansom-cab and a rosy mist.

Something must be said about that great coach and remarkable personality, W. L. Fletcher, the 'Flea'. Tall, lean, ruddy, with enormous shoulders, he was a rich bachelor who, when not coaching, travelled, ex-plored and shot big game. He had won a D.S.O. in the South African War. It was he who, when Cam-bridge rowing was in the doldrums in the late nineties, sportingly went to their help and produced several winning crews. His prestige and renown as a coach was great indeed. He did not rely for his success upon his genius for teaching the art of rowing. He lived with his crew ; he fathered and mothered us ; he kept up our morale, intuitively recognising each

F

man's individual necessities. He was a great smoker of
cigarettes, but gave up smoking indoors lest we, who
were forbidden it, might be made restless by the sight
and smell of tobacco. Naturally laconic to brusqueness,
he set himself to amuse and divert us at meals with
stories and reminiscence. He subdued his rather flinty
and prejudiced temper to his task of making a happy,
as well as a proficient, crew. Personally, when being
coached by the 'Flea', whether in a 'tub' or an Eight,
I was entirely dominated by him. All my accumulated
experience, all the instinctive movements through
which a practised waterman links blade to stretcher,
were forgotten. I tried to re-educate every muscle in
order to conform to his precise and complicated in-
structions. Instead of settling myself comfortably in
the boat, as I had been used to do, and allowing my
unconscious 'know-how' (as the Americans would say),
acquired through years of racing at Eton, to have its
head, I sat tremulously, as much out of touch with both
boat and water as any novice, trying to go through a
series of novel and exact motions. This was not what
the 'Flea' wanted, but it was what happened, and I
can only ascribe it to the extraordinary power of his
personality. I performed, under his eye, as one mes-
merised. De Havilland, at Eton, had been a great
coach, whom I had idolised, but never to the point of
abandoning the use of my own watermanship, made
instinctive through habit.

The following year 'Flea' again coached us, but we
turned out to be a worse crew than before, and had
the painful experience of being led all the way and
well beaten. When, in the summer, I was President
of the O.U.B.C., and invited the 'Flea' to be coach the

ensuing year, he refused. 'My coaching days are over,' he said. 'I have now reached a point where I have an ideal oar in my mind's eye. Nothing satisfies me except to turn each member of the crew into such an ideal oar, which is of course impossible. I have lost the knack of making the best of my existing material. I try to alter the material itself. I shan't coach again.' It was by far the longest speech I ever heard him make. I did not argue with him, for I knew that he was right. He had, with the best intentions, destroyed in my own case any chance I might have had of becoming a class oar, and there is some evidence, in the failure of the Oxford boat of 1906 to achieve any sort of uniformity or pace, that others had suffered in the same way.

In the autumn of that year the Trial Eights disclosed the great promise of J. A. Gillan (then 'Mary', now Sir Angus), and it was obvious that he, and not the President, was the right man for No. 5. 'Tarka' Gold, whom I had persuaded to coach, was the most tactful of men. It was for the President, not himself, to make up the crew, he said, but unless a place could be found for Gillan he did not see how he could conscientiously continue. I knew as well as he the right place for Gillan and had the exceptional, although not unprecedented, experience of kicking myself, as President, out of the Boat. It was the end of my rowing career, apart from the College Eights and Fours. It was hard at the time ; but 'Fluffy' Davis' undisguised pleasure at my return to sanity and books helped to console me ; and I was now free to coach the Balliol Torpid, and to have the satisfaction of seeing a young crew, in which three Eton dry-bobs, Julian Grenfell, Edward Horner and Victor Barrington-Kennett, rowed, make all their bumps before the 'Gut' and row Head of the River by an enormous margin. G. C. Bourne, in his standard work on Rowing, cites this Balliol Torpid as about the best fixed-seat crew in his long experience.

For one, like myself, now wholly dedicated to the Cult, and but lately High Priest, this triumph more than made up for the loss of the Presidency. Even the gentiles were prompt with their congratulations, for on returning from the river on the final afternoon to College, we found stuck up in the porch a picture, cut from some illustrated magazine, of naked savages dancing round a bonfire, and underneath the legend : 'Well rowed, Balliol !' (There were, incidentally, at Balliol, during my time, two high-caste Indians and one Japanese, but the pretence that we were a nest of Basutos and Hottentots was a never-failing pleasure to the pinkish or mottled races in other Colleges.) The members of that Torpid (whose Captain, rowing at bow, was the great K. N. Bell, then known as 'Keechey' after a favourite character at the Zoo) used oars whose handles had been shaved down to the slenderness that matched that of the oars of the seventies and eighties, which hung in the College Barge. I had found, by experiment, that if the fingers and thumb can all but meet round the oar-handle, the oarsman relaxes the muscles of forearm and wrist and is 'quicker into the water' at the beginning of the stroke. On a tip from Joe Legge, the parson-coach of Trinity, I also altered the length of the outriggers, so that the blades entered the water a little nearer to the fulcrum.

Joe Legge, who so generously advised me, although coaching a rival College, was an original character. His

trim red beard, flaming beneath his faded O.U.B.C.
cap, brightened the towpath like a traffic light. He was
a clergyman who had been suspended by his bishop for
preaching heretical sermons, for Joe laid more emphasis
upon charity than upon the Sacraments. I believe he
assisted, unpaid, in some Oxford parish, but he could
be found every evening at tea-time, in a corner of
Vincent's Club, talking wisely and pithily over the
muffins. Occasionally he would read his paper on
'Godless Morality' to some College Society. (He was,
like the preacher in the Calvin Coolidge chestnut,
'against it'.) Joe would have made a stimulating
College Chaplain if it had not been for bishops. As it
was, he eventually married, most happily, a barmaid.
No doubt his bishop said : 'I told you so'.

The earthly reward for good wet-bobs, the plum in
their pie, is Henley Regatta. To go from the Isis to
Henley is like a trip to Italy from a London February.
To spend a fortnight rowing on one of the loveliest
reaches in England in what seems to have been, in
retrospect, perpetual sunshine, without lectures or note-
books, sleeping on lawns in the afternoon heat, and
drifting down the river in a punt after twilight had
come, and the Fawley night-jars were hawking, four
or five together, overhead, was very heaven. If you
walked in the dusk, after a glass of port wine, to Ship-
lake or Wargrave, there was the scent of mown hay all
the way, and sudden pockets of air heavy with the
fragrance of sweet-briar, for there was no tarmac in
those days, nor any fumes of oil and petrol to blunt
the senses. The height of bodily fitness, and the good
company of a Balliol crew, enhanced the contentment.
Henley was undoubtedly the Promised Land for us

dedicated oarsmen, and it did not belie its promise. The College Barges, flowery and flagged, lined the Buckinghamshire bank ; delicious girls in picture-hats drooped with conscious grace in punts instead of crowding, as today, into a grand-stand ; canoes laden with minstrels swinging collecting-bags at the end of long poles, or with decorative sopranos in trailing muslins singing 'Vilja, oh, Vilja, the witch of the wood' nosed their way among the throng of boats ; and old 'Guts' Woodgate, in dirty white flannel trousers, side-whiskers and a speckled boater, commented from the towpath, in a voice that carried across the river, upon the degeneracy of the modern rowing man. And on the last night, when training was broken, we drifted downstream, 'flown with insolence and wine', seizing, with a cold wet hand, the ankle of a sleeping nymph in a private houseboat, or having a paddle-fight with a Cambridge gang who, hammering in vain at Bron Lucas' cork leg that hung over the side of a canoe, decided that Oxford men were insensitive to pain ; or, led by Alec Cadogan, a dry-bob guest, gate-crashing into Phyllis Court where the Mayor of Henley was giving a ball, and devouring, in dripping flannels amongst his tailed and white-tied guests, the mayoral quails and trifles. Insolence, yes, but a gay insolence, often turning aside, with mock commiseration and remorse, the victims' justifiable anger.

I sometimes wonder whether, had I myself — to suppose the impossible — become Head of an Oxford College, I should have continued in the rowing-religion in which I was nurtured. Or would maturity have inclined me to the views of 'Fluffy' Davis, who held that a man's years at Oxford were all too short for the serious business of learning, and that all games, rowing included, should be regarded purely as refreshment, like his own rather solemn lawn-tennis ? There were times enough, I must admit, in my last year at Oxford, when I felt the daily round of tubbing and coaching, as the only break in a nine-hour day of concentrated book-work, to be almost intolerable. As the imagined Head of a College, I must surely wish, I reflect, that my third- and fourth-year men should be spared that wearing grind. My College, I say to myself, will care nothing for its place on the River ; it shall be renowned for making 'fun', as each undergraduate sees it for himself, the proper object of recreation. Let them even 'cycle', like the sinful freshman of my own days, or fish, or botanise, or idle beneath the trees. The only test will be enjoyment and recreation in its true sense. And having satisfied myself of the reasonableness and good sense of this view of the matter, there comes a day in March when I open my *Times* to see a strange diagram on the sporting page : the chart of the Oxford Torpids. I hardly dare examine it, for fear that the Balliol Torpid has been bumped. At Henley, if a Balliol Eight or Four is competing, I follow the race with my very entrails. It is the same with an Eton crew ; it is the same with the Boat Race. Reasonableness and good sense are powerless against 'religious' loyalties (as I have found to my cost in other regards), and, on three or four occasions in each year, I am left in no doubt that, sensible or not, my subconscious self regards no effort, no drudgery too great, if it gives bumps to Balliol, a win at Mortlake to Oxford, and the Ladies' Plate to Eton. There seems to be only one, somewhat lame, solution for us rowing men : to go on serving the myth with fervour, but to smile, not unindulgently, at ourselves for doing so.

Balliol, as I have told, is not interested in Blues, except as useful members or coaches of the College crews. Inside the College walls the Presidency of the O.U.B.C. counted for nothing and I lost nothing by giving it up. In the University at large, however, the President had a certain prestige, and was the *ex-officio* Chairman of the Blues Committee, the ruling body in athletic manners. By coming to this post early in my second year, I unwittingly committed a solecism which caused some amusement. There was a celebrated Don at Hertford known as the 'Jacker' who had for years served the Blues Committee as Honorary Secretary, and by his experience, his enthusiasm and his permanency, had achieved an unofficial but *de facto* position of Athletic Dictator. I knew nothing of all this ; I do not think I had heard of the 'Jacker' until I attended a meeting of the Committee, mostly composed of third- and fourth-year Cricket, Rugger and Athletic Blues, and found myself in the Chair. The 'Jacker' as secretary sat on my left, busy with minute book and papers. We ran through some routine business. Then came an item on the agenda : 'Proposal to award a half-Blue for Water-polo'.

'A ridiculous suggestion,' I said, and crossed it out. There was a murmur of agreement, and we went on to the next item. When the meeting broke up I was surrounded by amused faces. 'Did you see the "Jacker's" face ?' I had not seen it, but it seemed that the proposal came from him, that he had already told the Water-polo players that they were to receive a half-Blue, and that never before had the 'Jacker's' motions been so much as opposed. So can green inexperience, by its very naïveté, sometimes defeat dictatorship. To the 'Jacker's' credit, he said never a word to me about the incident.

I had, when President, one glimpse of the persistence, even at Oxford, of the schoolboy's worship of athletes. I received a note from the President of a College J.C.R. personally unknown to me. He invited me to a Smoking Concert, adding : 'If you can come, we shall of course reserve a special chair for you in the middle of the front row'. I could only decline, thanking him, but pointing out that I was not the Prince of Wales.

It is often said, against rowing as a sport, that unlike most games, it is of no use to a man in after life. This is obvious enough, so far as actually rowing in a boat goes, but there are, I think, some habits formed by wet-bobs which stand them in good stead in middle life and beyond. There is, for example, the habit of suffering during the hours given to recreation. I remember my astonishment at hearing an athletic dry-bob declare that deer-stalking was too exhausting to be really enjoyable. I do not say that many dry-bobs would be capable of saying that, but I do affirm that no wet-bob could have said it. To ache, to be sore, to be blistered, to be exhausted, is all in the day's work for a rowing man, and when, in the sixties, he finds that he can no longer even garden without a pain in the back, well, that is only the sort of thing that he was brought up to.

Then again, there is the habit of being one of a crew. A cricketer can come glowing with pride and pleasure from a match in which his side was beaten, but the member of an Eight or Four, or even of a Pair, must inevitably share success or failure with the rest of the crew. And because of this, a wet-bob works by habit in a firm or partnership, or in any occupation where team-work is required, whereas a dry-bob must acquire that habit, perhaps painfully, and with moments of thirst for a century, or a hat-trick, be the form of his colleagues what it may. And lastly, the wet-bob is accustomed to not having any fun, and in this world of sinks and super-tax, a little fun has to go a long way.

Even so, had I to begin life again, and could find myself miraculously endowed with the capacity to hit a flying ball, I should plump for being a dry-bob. And if, as seems probable, my grandsons make the same choice, it will be with my full approval, until the day and the hour when I catch sight of the light-blue blades of an Eton Eight, or watch, from a house-roof in Chiswick Mall, an Oxford crew draw level with, then pass, then crack the Cambridge boat. For then reason and calculation will succumb to an inward illumination ; and who wants fun in the presence of glory ?

IV

The Quadrangle at Balliol, although spacious and well furnished with lawns for strolling, and shadowed, in summer, by trees more endeared to us for the men who sat beneath them than for any particular distinction of their own, is not beautiful. For the eye cannot rest upon lawn and tree, but is inevitably caught and held by the monstrous, neo-Gothic Hall. If it swivels round affrighted, the striped Chapel bars the way; if it tries to escape in another direction, there looms the grim Victorian-Tudor pile where 'Sligger' used to live. Only one corner comforts the fugitive eye: the angle made by the decent, well-bred, eighteenth-century Fisher's Buildings, in which the stairs led up to Cyril Bailey's consolatory rooms. (And even here, in spite of the agreeable sixteenth-century archway, and the Old Library in the corner of your eye, the glass door leading to the Master's lodging, and the bow-window of the Master's drawing-room, do petty outrage to Bishop Fisher's orderly and complaisant design.) There is extant a letter of Jowett's in which, referring to the newly-built Scottish Baronial building which contains the Main Gateway and fills two sides of the small Front Quad, he writes that at any rate it is 'beautiful'. One can fairly say of it that it serves the useful purpose of so numbing the sensibility of a visitor to the College, that by the time he reaches the Great Quad he is half-impervious to the lesser pain inflicted by its circum-ambient stones.

For all that, whenever Oxford comes into my mind, or I see 'Oxford' upon a printed page, it is not her towers and spires that I first envisage as seen in one precarious moment from the approaching train, nor the view from the Senior Common Room of the Queen's College, nor the gardens of St. John's or of New College in the month of May, nor Worcester, nor the piping of birds at dawn in Wadham Gardens, nor Magdalen Tower, nor the noble symmetry of Peckwater, but Balliol Quad. Perhaps it is only because I was lucky enough to live three years on Number XIV staircase, and that what I saw every day from my window is imprinted, by sheer frequency, upon my mind. But I prefer to believe that it is because Balliol Quad was the scene and the setting for the peculiar pleasures of our undergraduate lives ; for the lounging discussions, often under the stars ; for hob-nobbing with 'Sligger' and Cyril and Harold Hartley ; for Belloc's 'laughter and the love of friends' ; for rioting and song. It was our arena and our market-place, in which we shouted or whispered ; the Master walked there, stooping a little in his flowing gown ; and the young men, debouching in twos and threes from the Buttery after Hall, filled it with murmur and movement in the growing dusk.

But that is not to say that we Balliol men lived to ourselves, or were immune to the spell of Oxford at large. I have mentioned the dawn-chorus in Wadham Gardens. To hear that it was necessary to climb out

of College before sunrise, and to scale the Wadham
Garden walls. The great cedar of Wadham had been
disastrously broken by a May snowstorm a year earlier,
when we saved the Balliol elms by kicking footballs
into the branches all one afternoon, for the trees were
in full foliage, and could not support the weight of
snow. But the Wadham cedar, being evergreen,
should not have cared whether snow fell upon it in
May or December ; nevertheless it did care, and more
than one great limb fell off. It was to see the great
cedar that a party of us first visited those delectable
gardens. They were well guarded, for to visit them
it was necessary to pass through the Warden's own
Lodgings, and to write your name and College in a
copy-book, to which a pencil was attached by a string,
that lay upon a table in the passage. There were
several of us, and I came last, and to save time scribbled
'Jones' in the book, without initials. On our return
we were confronted by the Warden, lame little Dr.
Wells, looking displeased.

'Gentlemen,' he said, 'I did not think that men from
my own College, when taking advantage of a privilege,
would have sunk so low as to write "Jones" in my
book.'

I made a stiff little bow. 'Unfortunately for me,
sir, it happens to be my name.'

The Warden made a very low bow indeed. 'Sir,'
he said, 'I humbly beg your pardon.'

He made amends by inviting me to come when I
liked, and to disregard the book. This was the first
occasion in my life when I discovered that 'Jones' is
not always acceptable as a surname. When I became
engaged my future father-in-law gave the news to a

country neighbour, who first laughed, then said : 'And now tell me his real name'. At weddings and receptions of all sorts the lady reporters at the door drop their hands when I give my name, and the Travellers' Club on one occasion was not reported as having been represented at a Memorial Service because the Secretary, in spite of my warning as to what would happen, had insisted that I should be the Club's representative. Still, I have had a happy life. Perhaps the Warden's invitation was not really intended to cover a visit to his gardens at half-past three in the morning, and by way of the garden wall, but that is how a friend and I revisited it. The birds played up well ; but in dropping over the wall on my way home I just missed falling upon a policeman. He asked for my name and College, and, as I felt delicate about disclosing either, said that his orders were to accompany me to my College. I observed that this must be a thirsty job on so warm a night, and he agreed that it was so, but when I felt in my trouser-pockets I found I was penniless. I explained that if he would give me a leg-up over the much higher wall into Magdalen, I knew where to lay my hands upon half a crown. So it was a policeman who enabled me to burgle the rooms of my friend 'Evie' Southwell, who did not wake as I tiptoed to the dressing-table where his small change lay ; and the corrupt constable got his drink, and I went home unfollowed. I was never a scaler of walls, but repairs were being made to the back gate, and the scaffolding gave us, for a few weeks, an easy means of enjoying the scents and silence of a summer night.

'But Magdalen, lovely Magdalen, she was my mistress !' exclaimed Archbishop Lang at a Balliol

Gaudy, after telling us that All Souls had been his wife and Balliol his mother. I was too prudish in those days to share the Archbishop's voluptuous fancy about that lovely College, much as I admired the austere splendour of her eighteenth-century buildings in the deer-park, as well as her more celebrated Tower, and it was mainly to visit her rowing men that I so often went there. I even lived to get a welcome from 'Gunner', although I could never quite stomach bawdiness from a College servant. And at the Magdalen 'Afters' in the Junior Common Room I was a frequent guest. We sat at long tables eating candied fruits and almonds and drinking port, while all the acting talent in the University entertained us with songs and stories. Harry Tennent (who afterwards founded the famous firm of H. M. Tennent & Co. which today rules Theatreland) was the favourite star ; he had already a professional style, the showman's smile and nerve, and that mysterious inner certainty that all his turns are amusing, which distinguishes 'the real thing' from the amateur. He never failed to set the Magdalen tables on a roar and, as a dutiful guest, I roared with the rest ; but in my heart of hearts I felt what Gwennie Mars, in the immortal 'Follies', used to say, through her cold in the head, to Lewis Sidney : 'Doe, you're dot fuddy, bud you are a worker'. But nobody else, as far as I know, shared my lack of humour.

My port glass was freely replenished and lifted in turns, at the call of my name, to 'Bim' Gatehouse and Alister Kirby and 'Mary' Gillan and many other gay and gentle rowing giants, for the Magdalen boat was Head of the River and a Blue was a Blue in the Magdalen J.C.R. But, for all the cries of 'No heel-taps', I never had to be helped home. I had learnt my lesson, once and for all, in my first term, at the dinner of the Myrmidons in Merton. Tom Somers-Smith, my old partner in the Eton School Pulling, was my host, and 'Child' Stedall, who steered the Varsity crew, abetted him. I have to write 'abetted', for both were old hands among the Myrmidons, and must have known what was coming to me. We sat down to dinner in tail-coats, white ties and white waistcoats ; we were all 'Misters' during the soup and fish, and the champagne did no more than champagne should to make us talkative and loving-kind. But when the cloth had been taken away, and the decanters placed upon the mahogany, and the last of the College servants had noiselessly shut the door upon us, the serious business of the evening began, which was, as far as I can remember, the drinking of the healths of the guests. A port glass had to be emptied at each health ; I was afterwards told that I emptied twenty-four glasses. I did not go home unassisted, but even my assistant had to crawl most of the way from Merton to Balliol. I finally collapsed in 'the Jungle', that small island of shrubs that confronts the doorway of Number XIV. Here I was found, lifted and carried to bed by good friends. I was told that I had been first spied by Cyril Bailey who, a Good Samaritan in reverse, passed by on the other side. The miseries of that spinning night, and of the next day, have preserved me for life from drunkenness. Wise fathers will inoculate their sons, before sending them out into the world, with port ; it is, taken in excess, a poison which has such horrible results, even to the eye that sees its own yellowness in the shaving-glass, that nobody who has suffered from it will risk such suffering again. Not even the killing of Hector by the Myrmidons, in Shakespeare's version of that tragedy, could have been, since it was swifter, so brutal a handling as I got from the Myrmidons of Merton. Yet, manners being manners, I wrote a note to say how much I had enjoyed myself.

I frequented Merton, as I frequented Magdalen, primarily to talk to fellow wet-bobs, but there were other Colleges whose courts and gardens I haunted for their own sake. St. John's College was our neighbour, and though I had no acquaintance there, I feel to this day that a visit to Oxford, however brief, is incomplete if no respects have been paid to St. John's. There is an Italian delicacy in her arcades, and pools of ilex-shade beyond her Archery Lawn, that give one a sense on coming away that one has enjoyed a miniature holiday abroad, for all that her flower gardens are as English as they can be. At Professor Ball's lectures in St. John's there was a pretty girl, whom I never saw elsewhere. She was not merely pretty, she was seductive, but in a withdrawn, casual way, careful to meet no eyes with her own. Professor Ball lectured on Moral Philosophy, but at dictation speed, for he expected us to report him to ourselves *verbatim* in our note-books, and, since his lectures were very good indeed, those of us who were working seriously had few opportunities of watching the fascinating creature. But there is little doubt that Ball's lecture-room was so crowded because many who were not working seriously were drawn there as swarming bees to the Queen. Except for a few occasions in Eton Chapel, and once at a School Concert, this was my first experience of the extraordinary disturbance that a girl's face, even half-shadowed by a

G

hat-brim, even at no small distance, can work in a
gathering of young men.   There is yet another pretty
young woman entangled with my memories of St.
John's.   She was my partner at a Commemoration Ball
in Trinity, and I managed to get her over the wall into
St. John's, where another Ball was being held, and back
the same way.   We had a second, free supper in St.
John's Hall and I was rather proud of my performance,
because she wore a white satin frock, ankle length, and
somehow it remained spotless while I pushed or pulled
her up and down yew trees on either side of the wall.
She was an adventurous girl for those days, as well as a
pretty one ;   and I wish I could remember her name.
Nowadays, I am told, her partner would have kissed
her during such an escapade ;   in those days such
innocent pleasures were taboo.   Young women received
far more respect than they can ever, in their hearts, have
demanded or relished.

There were no girls to take us to Worcester, nor had
I friends there, but Senators are not the only people to
be taught, if not exactly wisdom, yet something which
is far from folly, by that surprising College.   I call it
surprising because Worcester has a stern and haughty
exterior that might have been painted by James Pryde,
turning, despite the perfection of its proportions, a
blank and discouraging stare upon the approaching
visitor.   But once inside the gate, and under the heavy
arcade, you get the most delectable of welcomes.   A
gracious, high-bred façade on your right looks down,
indulgently, at a row of irregular and diminishing little
houses on your left, with a lawn between ;   all is grace
and intimacy ;   there is neither condescension on the
right nor too much humility on the left.   A narrow

passage at the end of the little houses leads to wide lawns and great trees and a swan-lake, and I have known people who pretended to visit Worcester for the sake of these gardens. But lawns and trees and lakes are common enough ; it is the three-sided quadrangle, and the sudden pleasure of the transition from heavy, almost sullen blankness to smiling graciousness that gives to Worcester her incomparable charm. She lies remote from the rest, but has grandeur and elegance enough to make her self-sufficient. It is deplorable to think that we called her 'Wuggins'.

Magdalen, St. John's, Worcester, Wadham and the gardens of New College in lilac-time — these were our haunts on summer Sundays, for the majestic courts of Christ Church are shadeless and best visited when a low winter sun throws shadows even at noon. But the College that most caught my imagination, the mysterious, desirable, yet unattainable magnet for my ambitions, I never visited by day. For All Souls, that proud, aloof home of the elect, that will not stoop to housing or teaching undergraduates — unless you count a dozen legendary, obscure creatures called Bible Clerks whom nobody has ever seen or spoken to — All Souls keeps her gates locked. Fantastic pinnacles, such as you may see on the top of Milan Cathedral but nowhere else, stand guard about her smooth, unpeopled lawns ; gates and grilles allow you to contemplate, but never to enter, her silent precincts. She stands, a kind of Holy of Holies, at the very hub of the University, rubbing shoulders nowhere with the Town, and even appearing to shrug off, with her locks and keys, her limitrophe Colleges.

By night, I was on one or two occasions admitted to

All Souls. I even dined as the guest of Sir William Anson, the Warden, although I have no remembrance of how such a privilege can have come about. But I tasted the celebrated Audit Ale, served in small silver cups without handles, and sipped like port, not quaffed like ale. And, at the dessert taken in a separate chamber, I was talked to by Andrew Lang. He was no longer brindled, but all but white-haired, with dark brows and eyes, and a youthful look of eagerness. He told me, I remember, a ghost story — of a guest at Glamis who saw from his window a noiseless coach pass beneath it. The coachman looked up and stared at him — a cruel, foreign face that was imprinted on his memory. A year or more later, this guest was in a Paris hotel, waiting for the lift to take him to his room. The lift arrived and the liftman opened the gates. He had the face of the coachman. The guest recoiled, and stepped backwards, for the face was full of malignancy, and the lift ascended again without him. A few seconds later it crashed and all the occupants were killed. I certainly believed at the time that Lang himself thought the story authentic.

Andrew Lang is little remembered today, but in the nineteen-hundreds he was a literary lion, and I felt such elation at chatting companionably with him as would have been lately felt by a young man conversing with Sir Desmond MacCarthy. Lang had been a name to us even in our infancy, through the Blue Fairy Book, long before we knew anything about 'the surge and thunder of the Odyssey'. We must have had the 'Blue Fairy Book' in our hands at a very early age indeed, for I remember that my brother and I were so appalled at the picture of the Beast in 'Beauty and the Beast', with

consequent nightmares, that the book had to be put
away on a top shelf until we grew tougher. But later
we knew many of the stories almost by heart, and, in
meeting Andrew Lang, I had nursery memories, as well
as the thought of his 'dearness' to our hero R.L.S.,
to enhance the occasion. Unlike so many authors when
encountered in the flesh, he did not disappoint me at all.
His looks were more than equal to his fame.

On another occasion when dining in All Souls I
met Samuel Butcher, Lang's collaborator in translating
Homer. A quiet man of compelling charm, he talked
politics, not literature, and told how he had met Tim
Healy frothing in the lobby of the House of Commons,
and swearing that he would never speak to Mr. Balfour
again.

'But why, Tim ? What has A. J. B. done to you ?'

'He has just referred to me as "that person".'

'But if he did, hadn't you just called him a bloody
murderer ?'

'And why wouldn't I call him a bloody murderer ?
Isn't he an official ?'

I do not think that, on these privileged evenings, as
I looked about me, and followed my host from Dining
Hall to Common Room, and listened to strange stories
of the Warden, at esoteric rites, singing a song about a
Mallard, that I ever seriously considered the possibility
of a Fellowship for myself. But when I learned that
Fellows of All Souls received £250 a year for seven
years, with freedom, after one year of residence, to live
where they liked and to follow the occupation of their
choice, my ambition was fired. Here, I thought, was
the solution of our family problem : how was I to be
maintained while passing my Bar examinations, and

thereafter waiting for briefs ? For my father had declared, in his sweeping way, that when I went down from Oxford his resources would be exhausted, and I must somehow keep myself. An All Souls Fellowship was the answer. Thenceforward it was not the glory and distinction of a Fellowship that I thought about but the hard cash. It was with bread-and-butter, not academic, dreams that I gazed longingly through the grilles at those deserted lawns. And when, after a Second Class in Greats, thanks to 'Gammas' for Greek and Latin composition, I began in my fourth year to read History, A. L. Smith himself began to talk about All Souls, at first as a star to which to hitch my wagon, but later on, too confidently, as something well within my grasp. So it is not surprising that after he and 'Fluffy' Davis had succeeded, after a year of grind, in getting me a First in the History Schools, and a good one, I began to think that £250 a year for seven years as no longer a dream, but a possibility. It began to obsess my mind as the supreme test for myself of success or failure in life ; with it, I could have a career at the Bar and a happy issue for a preposterous but devastating love affair ; without it, I should drift into private tutoring or some other form of aimless and celibate penury. It was no wonder that I ground away until all my nights were restless with dreams of perpetual essay-writing, and that when I came up after Schools for the Viva, the examiners, as one of them afterwards told me, had not the heart to question a candidate with so green and worried a face. I was none the less congratulated on my papers, a traditional sign of a First, and I had no tremors when the telegram arrived from Hancock. But the pressure had to be kept up until the examination for All Souls in late October. I was soundly beaten by Hulton, a dark horse from New College, a young man who, having passed first into Woolwich and been rejected on medical grounds, began for the first time to learn Greek, and in two years got a First in Mods, followed by a First in Greats. He, too, was killed in the war. It was well for All Souls that I did not come up against mediocrity and scrape a Fellowship, for it has been evident to me ever since that my success in the Schools was a mere flash in the pan, the result of expert cramming, and that I have never been of the mental calibre to maintain the lustre and prestige of that distinguished place.

I was staying with my parents' friend 'Dick' Strutt, at Rayleigh House in Chelsea, when the hateful telegram arrived, to undo me. We were in the middle of luncheon, and, fortunately for me, my father, ever incapable of disguising his feelings even in company, groaned aloud. That audible moaning saved me. 'Now', I said, reaching for the cream-jug, 'I can enjoy this superb apple-tart.' And I believe I did enjoy it ; if only to rebuke the lack of starch in my father's upper lip. All the same, it was a melancholy walk we had together, that dreary November afternoon, up and down Chelsea Embankment. My father, in his disappointment, took the line that we must now face it that, while not morally at fault, I was a failure. We must readjust our ideas of my future. He could no longer afford to give me an allowance. He supposed that, in spite of failing for All Souls, I might be able to obtain a post as tutor or bear-leader to some small boy. Meanwhile I could work for the Bar in my spare time ; we must hope that Law would prove to be more within my capacities, now proved to be so meagre, than History.

Beyond pointing out, quite irrelevantly, that Hilaire Belloc had failed for All Souls, I had nothing to say. I had always argued freely and easily with my father on any question in the world but one — that of money. I had never been for long, whether at Eton or Oxford, unconscious of the strain I was causing to the family resources. Having failed in my attempt to relieve that strain, I felt myself to be, entirely and with all justice, in my father's hands. I agreed that I must look for a tutorship. I did not relish the prospect. I felt as I used to feel at Eton on wet Tuesdays, with 'long school' in the offing. I left London that evening for a few days' pheasant-shooting on the Berkshire downs. Several of my fellow-guns knew that I had been in for All Souls, said cheerfully, 'Hard luck !' and treated me exactly as before. When I returned to London I found that a complete change in the family weather had taken place. My mother had been, once again, explaining life to my father. He was in high spirits. I was to have the same allowance as before ; I was to find my own 'digs' with my own friends while working for the Bar ; I had proved by my success in the Schools that I should one day be Lord Chancellor. Having escaped falling so low, my own spirits could not rise so rapidly as my father's. I got over it, as one gets over everything, but for long years I could not think or hear of All Souls without that little, private, fleeting moment of misery that Adam must have felt, even when he was over nine hundred years old, even with Eve's hand in his own, at some tactless mention of Eden. But Adam had at least been a Fellow of Eden once upon a time ; the place which I felt myself uniquely fitted not indeed to deserve or to adorn, but to savour and to enjoy, neither had been nor ever would be mine. And today, at this very moment, as I write 'All Souls' upon this page, I can detect a tiny, evanescent, but quite indubitable pricking in my heart.

Another College that I visited from time to time was Lincoln ; not for its beauty, but to learn about the Romans from W. Warde Fowler. I think it must have been when Strachan-Davidson was wintering in Egypt, but whatever the reason I had the privilege for a term of sitting *tête-à-tête*, one evening a week, with that fascinating man. He sat by the fire in a low arm-chair, and, because of his deafness, I sat on a stool almost at his knee, the coffee-cups on a low table between us. He had a thatch of thick white hair, and very fine cameo-like features ; he spoke in the low, level tones of the very deaf. He had manners of the utmost simplicity, and treated me not as a pupil, the burdensome object of an hour of professional duty, but as a guest to be entertained. If, after preliminary chat about the marsh-warblers at Kingham or the last Sunday concert in Balliol Hall, we fell into a discussion of the character of Tiberius, it seemed to be more by accident than because I was reading Roman History for Greats. 'Poor chap,' he would say, 'he never got over Vipsania' ; and I felt that Warde Fowler must have been there, a casual and compassionate spectator from the opposite side of the narrow Roman street, on the occasion when the youthful Tiberius, by pure mischance, caught sight once again of his dear Vipsania, and followed her with eyes of such hopeless yearning — 'adeo tumentes oculos'. And those Senators, Julia's

gang, flattering and toadying him with hatred in their
hearts — 'one can't wonder he felt like hitting back at
them . . . a plain old-fashioned soldier as he was . . .
bit of a ram-rod, of course' — Warde Fowler seemed
to be musing aloud, reminiscing about old acquaintances
rather than cramming a young man for the Schools.
And all this, the bright fire, the arm-chairs, the leisurely
relaxed 'tempo', stretching one hour to two, was
lavished by this friendly man upon a single undergraduate from another College ! Is it any wonder that
Warde Fowler has a place in my memories very close
to that of Strachan-Davidson himself, and that an
Oxford in which learning could be got so cosily, and
from men so rare, has held me continuously spellbound ?
Another Don who admitted myself and many Balliol
men to his friendship was C. R. L. Fletcher, the
historian. I was never his pupil — perhaps he had
retired to write his *History of England* — but we used
to lunch or sup with him in North Oxford, or perhaps
walk round the Parks on a Sunday afternoon. His son
George, an Eton Colleger, known as 'Hôj', was my
contemporary at Balliol and rowed in the College
Eight ; a rugged, humorous, pithy character who had
his own view of things, and was as well-met in the
Quad as any man of my day. A likely future Head-
master of Eton, but for the war ; he and his younger
brother were both killed. George and his father talked
together like friends, and we were lucky indeed to
become, through George, on easy terms with that
stimulating man. He had an Irish terrier to whom he
was much attached, the only dog I ever knew to be a
Secretary. He was Secretary to the North Oxford
Dogs' Club, but gave his master a good deal of anxiety

thereby. For he lacked the gift of continence and took advantage of his position to debauch the wives and daughters of the other members of the N.O.D.C. But he was a dog of charm and character, and got away with it.

'Breezy' is an adjective generally reserved for Admirals, not Dons, but it does fit Charles Fletcher. In after years, when I was married and staying at Howick with my wife's family, Fletcher came over to lunch. There stood in the dining-room at Howick an immense eighteenth-century screen. 'Ah,' exclaimed Fletcher as he entered the room, 'there is the very screen behind which Charles Grey seduced the Bishop of Durham's wife !' It was the first my father-in-law had heard of this escapade by his celebrated grandfather, Reform-Bill Grey, and he must have wondered, I think, which of the pair, Mrs. Barrington or Lord Grey, had mentioned the screen, and to whom. But historians are supposed to know these things, and the Whig-dogs were addicted, in their day, to more than one kind of liberty ; so my father-in-law laughed it off, with that enchanting laugh of his. But when, later still, I became a partner of Bernie Barrington and told him the tale, he said no Bishop's wife, still less a Barrington's wife, could have permitted such a thing, screen or no screen, and he refused to call my wife cousin.

V

ONCE a week, on Sunday evenings, Balliol Hall became a receptacle for all the music-lovers in Oxford, male and female. Those who have frequented concert-halls will know that one of Nature's most kindly whims has been to compensate the ill-favoured by implanting in them a love of good music. Nature's concert-goers are gnome-like or fish-like, with myopic eyes and exaggerated Adam's apples, and I owe much to Cyril Bailey for persuading me not to be intimidated by the outward appearance of the crowd that thronged the steps of Hall, but to try to share, as far as I might, their enviable sensibilities. Besides, he pointed out, the gallery was reserved for Balliol undergraduates, and it was from the gallery that I got my first taste of chamber music and the classics.

The moving spirit in those Balliol concerts fifty years ago was Dr. Ernest Walker. Thin, bent, etiolated, with a despondent black beard and a falsetto voice, Dr. Walker looked anything but the 'live wire' that he, in fact, was. I was one of the Master's dinner-party on a Sunday evening when he escorted his guests, as was his custom, to the middle of the front row. His principal guest was the irrepressible old Irish Lord Chancellor, Lord Ashbourne, who had been plainly reluctant to abandon the Master's port for an hour of high-brow

music. Ernest Walker was to open the programme
with a Beethoven Sonata and sat at the piano a few
feet from Lord Ashbourne, waiting for silence. The
old Irishman went on talking. Dr. Walker fixed him
with a hostile and impatient eye, hands raised, wrists
drooping above the keyboard, like a dog begging. In
the silence of the expectant Hall, Lord Ashbourne's
voice rang out :

'That young man looks as if a glass of woine would
do him good.'

Ernest Walker continued to eye the speaker,
unmoved.

'Oi fancy he would loike us to stop conversing,'
added Lord Ashbourne, as loudly as before, but turning
to the Master. The Master made a sign of assent ; Lord
Ashbourne settled himself in his chair ; the thin, pale
hands stopped drooping, pounced, and the concert
began.

I was too junior to have known Donald Tovey, most
erudite of Balliol musicians, although on one occasion,
after some festivity in Hall at which he was guest, he
went to the piano on the dais and performed some of
his famed musical parodies. He had a great head,
expanded, one felt, with learning, but in other respects
I should have taken him for a jolly, fat, easy-going
farmer. He could have blown Ernest Walker into a
corner with his laugh. But I did know F. S. Kelly —
'Clegg' — more celebrated as a sculler than musician
during his short life. He was killed in the war, and
those who know have told me that, had he lived, he
would surely have made his mark as composer. A. L.
Smith used to attribute the perfection of Clegg's
movements in a sculling-boat to his innate musicianship,

and 'A. L.' may well have been right, for rhythm is of
the essence of good sculling, and Clegg's strong pianist's
wrists and sensitive touch must have had their part in
the economy and punctuality of his consummate blade-
work. Clegg won the Diamond Sculls many times
and held the record for many years ; I still remember
the bored expression with which he raced, and the
lovely precision with which body, hands, slide and legs
moved in unison throughout the stroke, to rest together
for a split second before the recovery. On land,
curiously enough, he was a little clumsy.

Clegg had no manners and could be disconcerting
at a first acquaintance, blurting out home-truths and
treading on toes, but he had a warm and hospitable
heart, and his cool and stately sister, who shared his
riparian home at Bisham, more than made up with her
friendly, civilised ways for Clegg's abruptness. They
were a devoted pair ; Maisie knew how to protect a
guest from Clegg's irritation at the guest's failure to
grasp whether his host was talking of puppies or of
poppies (for he pronounced both words alike) without
letting her brother down. But when dinner was over,
and Clegg went to the piano, the lazy disdain, as well
as the flash of impatience, went out of his face, and he
was all ardour and flame.

Clegg had gone down from Balliol before I went
up, but I might have had a link with the musical world
through my exact contemporary 'Ferdy' Speyer, had
he not put his fiddle away in order to make a name for
himself in the soundless spheres of Nitrates and Food
Production. Ferdy had music in his blood, and won
the Nettleship Scholarship, and we, who knew nothing
about fiddling but crowded the gallery of Hall when

Ferdy was to play, foresaw a future in which we should be occasionally stared at when supping with the Maestro at a small, intimate table, after some great musical occasion. But Ferdy's standards were so high, and his taste so fastidious, that he developed private doubts as to whether he would indeed reach a professional level acceptable to his pride, for in artistic matters Ferdy is an aristocrat and makes no concessions, to himself least of all. I do in fact sit at small intimate tables with him, but it is beneath fifteenth-century arcades at Poppi, or Montepulciano, where nobody stares. And I do not, if I can help it, go to concerts with him, for musicians detect faults where the rest of us are enraptured, and it is depressing to be told that your raptures were out of place, since the second movement was taken too fast, and the oboes were ragged. In music, to a far greater degree, I think, than in any other art, the gap between initiate and layman is enormous ; musicians hear things that we others cannot even guess at, and although those Balliol concerts did first show me a pleasure that has been lifelong and increases as the years go by, it is not, I am sure, an enjoyment that any true musician would cross a street to share.

But if music was, by its very nature, out of bounds to many of us, there was nothing to stop us getting on intimate terms with books except lack of time. The Schools prompted all our reading, and when 'Fluffy' Davis made me read *Esmond* and, strange to say, *Romola*, as being handmaidens to History, I felt towards him as one feels to a doctor who prescribes fresh air instead of the potent shot in the arm one had hoped for. All the same 'Tally' (now Sir Stephen Tallents) used to carry

A Shropshire Lad in the pocket of his Norfolk jacket, and attempted to make co-devotees of us in the Quad before he went off to play poker with Percy Perryman. I was always embarrassed when 'Tally' pulled out his *Shropshire Lad*, because I could not then, and cannot now, bow down before that minor classic. There are lines, yes, even a whole stanza here and there, of grace and beauty, perfect in their pointful economy. But, taken as a whole, I found and find the little volume wishy-washy. 'Tally' had most of literary England with and behind him, and my embarrassment was at discovering that I was so lacking in poetic sensibility as to be bored with those Lads and their pathos. One of the pleasures of being seventy is no longer to care about not caring for what all the world commends.

Against that, one of the pleasures of being an under-graduate is to enjoy literary dishes too tough for the Common Reader, and we were fortunate in having Meredith, at the height of his vogue, to devour. One really did need good teeth for the preface to *The Egoist*, or for *The Woods of Westermain* and while, in my own case, I still rank him high as novelist and higher yet as poet, it is in despite of the obscurity that we once almost gloried in, as I suppose the young men of today glory in the wilful opacities of *Faber's Book of Modern Verse*. Meredith certainly was wilful ; he could write *Prince Lucifer* when in the vein, as well as *Evan Harrington*, but if his poetry almost invariably profits by lucidity, it is not so with his novels. So brilliant a comedy is *The Egoist* that I once thought half-seriously of translating it into English, for the delight of thousands who cannot be bothered to cope with the language in which it is written. But I saw in no time that it would

never do. You cannot de-meredithise, as the Home
Office would say, that extraordinary work of art. Clara
and Vernon might survive in plain English, but Sir
Willoughby and Laetitia Dale would crumble into
nothingness. They are the creatures of phrase-making,
articulated with aphorisms and fleshed with convoluted
verbosity. But they triumph, all the same. I can still,
on re-reading, feel the excitement as the ring closes, as
the victim wildly dashes this way and that, until, in the
final moment of abject surrender, all one's scorn and
derision turns to something not far from pity. *Evan
Harrington* and *Rhoda Fleming*, written in straightforward prose, have not half the 'bite' of that tortured
and torturing comedy.

So we capped verses from *Modern Love* or from
Phoebus with Admetus, and I privately enrolled *The Day
of the Daughter of Hades* among my favourite bed-
fellows. And to show our mettle, we read *Richard
Feverel* and *Beauchamp's Career* and *Vittoria* and *Sandra
Belloni* from cover to cover, and quarrelled with Eric
Romilly for putting *Shagpat* above them all. But
intrepid as we were, not one of us ever finished *One of
our Conquerors*, and I can hardly suppose that anyone
else has finished it either. It is curious to reflect, when
considering our appetite for the involved and the complicated, that in these years a Mr. Henry James was, for
me, 'a delightful American novelist' with whom a
golfing aunt at Rye occasionally took tea. I never
heard his name mentioned in the Quad.

Keats I discovered during a Long Vacation spent in
Norfolk, and got the Odes by heart through keeping
the book in a rustic earth-closet among the laurels of
the Mill House at Costessy. (I had a moment of

H

genuine pride late in life on learning that a distinguished
critic kept one of my books of light verse in a com-
parable place.)   But it was at Balliol, during a Christmas
vacation, when I stayed 'up' for special coaching by
A. L. Smith, and got less of his attention than I had
expected owing to a hard frost which kept that enthusiastic skater all the hours of daylight on the flooded
Christ Church Meadows — it was in my icy bedroom
and a silent and deserted College that I first opened
The Oxford Book of French Verse.   If I did not open it
at Victor Hugo's 'Booz' I certainly came to that miracle
soon enough, and learnt to what heights of sonority and
grace the French language can attain.   To my ignorance
'Booz' was a revelation and the first reading of it an
event, and I still think the poem contains the most
exquisite stanzas known to me in French.

Walter Pater was still the fashion in my Balliol days,
and *Marius the Epicurean* stood on many bookshelves,
but it was wonderful how fresh and virginal the volumes
managed to appear in their unfingered bindings.   The
insistent search for beauty of expression has its dangers
for a writer of prose ; the crevasses of preciosity yawn
about his path, and his matter tends to become attenu-
ated, if not lost, behind the veil of his manner.   I was
told that *Marius* was to be admired, and I made an
honest attempt to admire, but I got bogged in the
clinging, cloying 'beauty' of Pater's style.   But his
essay on Pico di Mirandola did open a new door to me,
and give me my first glimpse of the Renaissance.   Pater
needed, I think, a factual subject to keep his feet on the
ground ; his own creations ran away with him.   So
I always felt uneasy when Pater was being discussed,
and had to take refuge in my alternative capacity of

beefy rowing-man, who could not be expected to join
in the talk. And it was no surprise to me when, years
later, I found my second volume of *Marius* still uncut.

Another, and very different, 'fashion' of those days
was for Anatole France. I believe I began with *L'Île
des Pingouins* lent to me by Ferdy Speyer, whose nose
for irony was and remains as sharp as a nib. But
'Fluffy' Davis himself read a paper on France to the
Dervorguilla Society, and I remember to this day my
indignation when Orlo Williams rose in the debate and
declared that the cat 'Hamilcar' was a bore. Since then
a whole generation of Frenchmen have gone further
than Orlo, and declared Anatole France himself to have
been a bore and a charlatan. Can such a judgment
have been one small symptom of that malady which
led to 1940 ? Perhaps a reader must be at peace with
himself to enjoy limpid, lucid prose for its own sake ;
perhaps only those who still trail wisps of innocence can
appreciate the simplicities of a Jacques Tournebroche or
the tarnished, intermittent virtue of his good master
the Abbé Coignard. If the author himself was far from
admirable, so was Laurence Sterne, and if Parson Yorick
and My Uncle Toby are the immortal children of a
bad Christian, the endearing saints and sinners of an
agnostic transgressor have an equal claim, I think, to
endure. For sheer wit and delicacy of irony France
can surely be placed abreast of Sterne ? However that
may be, in the first decade of this century Anatole
France fitted our humour like a glove, and, Dons and
undergraduates alike, we swapped enthusiasms and
capped quotations from *Le Procurateur de Judée*, *Le Livre
de Mon Ami*, or *La Rôtisserie de la Reine Pédauque*.

There have been hints of late that Anatole France is

to enjoy what the world of sport and entertainment calls a 'come-back', and it may be that his paper-covered volumes, with the admirable large type on greyish, rough-edge pages, are once more left lying beneath the Balliol trees on summer days. But is it conceivable that a copy of *Middlemarch* could be discovered today in the bookshelves of any undergraduate ? I have told how my history tutor ordered *Romola* as holiday reading ; present-day undergraduates are fortunate in that no such command could be given to them, nor would they, I suspect, be docile enough to obey if it were. But when Bill Farrer and Chris Goschen joined in refusing to believe their ears at my admission that I had not read *Adam Bede* ('I always thought Adam Bede was a woman', whispered Lord Haig to his A.D.C. after seeing the tomb of the Venerable Bede at Durham) or heard of Mrs. Poyser, I made haste to rehabilitate myself, for both of them knew what was what. But it was *Middlemarch*, not *Adam Bede*, that they should have exclaimed about. A novel published in 1871 that one and the same man reads with pleasure in 1905, with admiration in 1935, and with both in 1955, must be wearing well enough to deserve the name of 'classic'. If *Middlemarch* is not to be found in Balliol today, then somebody should leave a copy on the bench by the mulberry tree.

It is strange, as I have said, that Henry James meant no more to me than the nodding acquaintance of an aunt at Rye, but it is stranger still that the works of one whose shoe-latchet James was only just worthy to loose should have been unknown to most of us. For Joseph Conrad had already published *Lord Jim* and *The Nigger of the Narcissus*, and the massive, heart-searching

Nostromo, as well as *Youth* and some minor works. Just as the socially and politically conscious parts of me find it hard to recapture the ethos of a period when war was the business of soldiers and sailors alone, so the book-loving part of me can with difficulty recall a time when Conrad was not upon my shelves, a giant with whose stature to measure and compare all new-comers in English fiction. Against whom did we pit the rising author in those days ? Not against Meredith, for he was *sui generis*. Not against our dear Kipling, for he was a story-teller, not a novelist. Stevenson ? Except for *Weir of Hermiston*, there was always a 'book-for-boys' feel about his novels, in spite of their craftsmanship. It must have been, I suppose, against Thomas Hardy. *Tess* and *Jude* and *Far from the Madding Crowd* were already classics, for all that their author, like Meredith, was still living. It was a Balliol Prime Minister whose Balliol private secretary rang up Buckingham Palace, on the occasion of Hardy's seventieth birthday, and suggested that a royal telegram to 'old Hardy' might be appreciated. 'Jolly good idea,' was the reply, 'it shall be done', and Mr. Hardy of Alnwick, renowned maker of fishing-rods, was astonished to receive royal congratulations on attaining an age he had not attained on a day which was the anniversary of nothing. But this is digression. Hardy we did read and enjoy, inclined, as young people are, to give undue preference to *Jude* as a reward for its un-Victorian starkness.

I have just written 'our dear Kipling', and it is melancholy to me to realise that no Balliol under-graduate of today could conceivably call Kipling 'dear'. How did it come about that the one-tenth Jingo in the make-up of that gifted man has been allowed to swamp the nine-tenths artist ? In the sheer telling of a short story he has few, if any, equals, nor can he easily be matched in the art of imposing verisimilitude upon the creations of the imagination. It was no mere beater of imperial drums who wrote *Wireless* or *The Finest Story in the World* or *They* or *The Tomb of his Ancestors*. Is *Kim* the work of a race-proud Sahib who regarded all Indians as 'niggers' ? Is *Recessional* the verse of a braggart ? Are *The Jungle Books* and *Puck of Pook's Hill* calculated to turn our children into hammers of the heathen ? You might think it, if you were to go by the verdict of many a modern. The explanation of Kipling's eclipse can only be that those who decry him have not troubled to read him. And since he is the most readable of men, they have no excuse for their laches.

Kipling could, once in a while, be dull about Freemasons ; he could be tasteless ; his humour was sometimes 'Third Form' humour ; it was better not to meet him in the flesh (he once visited another College in my time and appalled a gathering of young admirers by telling them smutty stories) ; but a writer, like any other artist, must surely be judged by his ascents, not by his occasional falls. If young people today say they have the short stories of Mr. Somerset Maugham, and so have no need of Kipling's, I can only reply that Mr. Maugham has craftsmanship and invention, but that Kipling had, in addition to these, imagination of the rarest kind, often laced with poetry. And he never lost his relish, and a boyish wonder at things. It is enjoyment, not disenchantment, that endears a writer to his readers. I am positive that memory was not tripping me up when I wrote 'our dear Kipling'. Does this generation, will any generation, write about 'our dear Maugham'?

I was much too busy working for Schools to read *The Old Wives' Tale* when it first came out, although I can remember the stir it made, but many of us delighted in a first novel by Mr. William de Morgan, a young writer of sixty-six, with its gorgeous opening. *Joseph Vance* is little heard of nowadays, and perhaps I was too easily pleased when old Vance fought the man for crocking the bloody little insec' he found in his beer, but I am sure it was an artful, truthful tale that rolled out, leisurely and mellow, to make us believe that a new writer of 'class' had appeared.

In attempting to portray the minds and habits of one generation of Balliol undergraduates, irrelevancies ought to be discarded ; but it would be ungrateful of me not to recall a private pleasure, not shared with many, that I owed to the lady who wrote under the *nom de guerre* of 'Lanoe Falconer'. Mary Hawker, granddaughter of the celebrated Colonel Hawker, whose book on shooting was a minor classic in its day, lived at Longparish in Hampshire, and her neighbour Eveline, Lady Portsmouth, was said to have been the original 'Cecilia de Noël' in the fascinating ghost story of that name. It is a work of art, perfect in detail as a conversation-piece by Zoffany, exhibiting a small gallery of portraits, serious or comic, so alive and exact as to be unforgettable and with its unashamed sentiment so artfully dressed up in humour as to be wholly acceptable. Those who have no acquaintance with Atherley and Lady Atherley and the Canon and Mrs. Mallet the Cook, should make haste to meet them, but the tryst will have to be in a second-hand bookshop. The story was already, in my day, a little old-fashioned, with a ghost appearing among hip-baths and hot-water cans, and although I liked to give the book as a wedding present within my means, I do not remember any effusive thanks. But I still think that the tale wears well, and while I do not recommend it to those who refresh themselves with *Finnegan's Wake*, it would have been a shabby thing to pass it by unnoticed. Lanoe Falconer may be forgotten, but not by me, and her niche in English letters, however exiguous, holds the figure of an artist.

VI

My second Christmas vacation was spent with my family in Rome. My father had taken a flat warmed only by open fires of fir-cones and logs ; there was a hard frost during the whole of our sojourn, and there was a moment every day when I bitterly criticised Augustus, who found a city of brick and left a city of marble, for starting a fashion which was followed even by the makers of lavatory-seats. In ten degrees of frost marble can inflict more cruel punishment than a birch-rod. And since I was now an Oxford man and no longer a schoolboy, I should have liked to have been on my own, that first brilliant morning on the steps of the Piazza di Spagna, when the flower-girls fluttered round me, like peacock butterflies about a buddleia, and stuck posies into the lapels of my coat. For they were prettier girls than I had ever seen, with ways as pretty as themselves, and I secretly wished that I could have relaxed the stiff, indifferent poker-face imposed upon me by my mother's company. I think my mother must have been feeling thankful that she was by my side, to judge from the peremptory way she shooed the creatures off ; or was the temptation she feared no more than that of extravagance, the perennial preoccupation of us all ? At any rate I bought no flowers, and re-marked what a nuisance those girls were, to buy off any suspicion my mother might have had that I thought them perfect darlings, as I did.   When, many years later, my mother chaffed me about my attitude towards young women, saying : 'I am always expecting to hear you speak of the loveliest girl as "that young person"', I realised the opacity of the protective wall I had raised between her and myself on this question of girls. Although rarely undisturbed by one charmer or another, I had used the bricks baked by childhood's hypocrisy with such effect as to baffle even a mother's eye.   I am glad to think that at long last, when it came to real business, she was my trusted confidante, as her heart so richly deserved.   But among the flower-girls, in that Roman sunshine, I should have liked to be alone.

I was still in the early days of reading for Greats, but had been sufficiently coached by Cyril Bailey for this Roman visit to realise the privilege it was to be taken round the Forum by Commendatore Boni himself.   The earth beneath the 'niger lapis', the black stone, had been lately excavated, and we descended into a narrow pit, and the Commendatore removed some damp sacking and showed us, still *in situ*, a small, dark conical stone on which was inscribed what may have been an early Roman or Etruscan criminal code. It was all very cramped and frustrating at the bottom of that hole, cluttered with boards and beams, but I managed to be genuinely thrilled, and to feel the cold dreadness of the penalty : *sakros esto*, 'let him be sacred'.   To be 'taboo', untouchable : one wondered what, in practice, that doom might be ?   How ancient is the ambivalence of the idea of sanctity, covering on the one hand the object too holy to be handled, on the other the thing you wouldn't touch with a barge-pole ?

The French have preserved the double sense in *sacré* ;
are we doing the same when we say 'my sacred aunt' ?
or only when we call the child a 'holy terror' ?

Above ground, I must own that there was too little
of the Forum to satisfy me ; I had seen the few still
upright columns in those enlarged photographs that
hang in so many Eton pupil-rooms, and had always
hoped that there might be more round the corner. But
there were not. To Commendatore Boni, and to Mr.
Ashbee, pale and melancholy, with whom we also had
the privilege of visiting so little where there had once
stood so much, there is no doubt that the Forum
appeared in its crowded pristine grandeur. Their inward eyes saw columns sprouting from the ground, or
'falling in' like foot-guards, to front or to flank the
temples and the basilicas, the curia and the colonnades.
But I, not being a Joachim du Bellay, saw only with
the outward eye, and saw little but a waste, irregular
plot, strewn with irrelevant stones and scarred with the
raw ulcers of recent excavations. I knew too little to
imagine more, but just enough to be disappointed.
Mr. Ashbee accompanied us to Livia's House, of which
I remember nothing but square lead pipes and flat
bricks stamped, as sharply as if but a week ago, with
the maker's name. A die had been used for the stamp-
ing, and I recollect wondering how it was that, having
made a die to impress seven or eight letters at a jab,
the Romans never thought of a separate die for each
letter, so inventing the moveable type for which the
world had to wait fifteen centuries. Since they wrote
by pressure upon wax tablets, the literary use of a
press would not have required any gigantic leap of the
imagination, and while waxen books would have been

impracticable, some child would surely, playing with
the dies, have sooner or later thumped a muddied one
upon his small brother's linen smock.

This visit to Rome was fifty years ago, and I have
not been there since, so that my impressions are discrete
and disorientated. But you cannot see Rome at twenty,
under that blueness of sky that goes with a sharp windless frost, without the kind of exhilaration that, on
passing, leaves you a little less of a Boeotian, a little
nearer to an Athenian, than before. The remains of
ancient Rome did, because of my unprepared mind,
excite me less than I had hoped, for all my admiration
of these lordly fragments of aqueduct strung at ragged
intervals across the brown Campagna, among the
umbrella pines. I was enchanted, it is true, with the
delicate perfection of the round temple of Vesta — as
it was still wrongly called in those days — and of her
other temple at Tivoli ; where I learnt for the first
time the heavenly, liberating effects of drinking a rough,
red wine in the middle of the day. For although I had
become talkative and affectionate on champagne and
mulled claret at Balliol and Pixton, I had never before
experienced the rosy, cosy haze that can so enhance the
happiness of an Italian afternoon, making the mountains
nearer, and the cypresses dearer. But the real thrill for
me, the pleasure for which I had been so little prepared
that it carried the excitement of discovery, was my first
acquaintance with the ecclesiastical architecture of the
middle centuries, from Romanesque to Baroque. I
had seen the great Norman arches in Norwich Cathedral
carried on rounded towers rather than columns ; but I
had never seen the delicacy of a cloister such as that of
San Paolo fuori Muri, where grace and slenderness

uphold and endure with no visible signs of strength.
Few names come back to me — is Santa Maria in
Cosmedin the church whose columns, every one, are
borrowed from Ancient Rome ? — but I was young
and tireless and went from church to church, surfeiting
my empty sensibilities, hitherto sparsely furnished with
pointed Gothic, on arch and column and vaulting, on
cloister and arcade.   There were momentary distractions : nuns in blue and white robes, seen through a
golden grille, who came sweeping in with downcast
looks to kneel and chant divinely, in a high-set church
approached by a flight of stairs ; or Cardinal Rampolla,
whose head would have embellished a Roman coin,
processing beneath a canopy in, I think, Santa Maria
Maggiore, and showing no sign of chagrin at having
been lately passed over in favour of Pius X.   For the
Emperor Franz-Joseph had exercised his imperial veto,
as I had been told, because Rampolla had appeared at
the Opera House in Vienna accompanied by his mistress,
a freedom the Emperor himself would not have pre-
sumed to take ; and I was thrilled to think that this
magnificent figure, whom I could have touched by
stretching out an arm, was a living copy of the worldly,
self-forgiving prelates of the Renaissance.   The story
was doubtless told me by a Protestant and may have
been quite unfounded ; but I was a puritan in those
days, and like all puritans pleasurably excited by the
propinquity to a reputed rake, and I would have liked
to have had a companion earthy enough to share the
experience.   With my family, chaster in thought than,
on looking back from this age, appears quite human, it
could not be shared.   With another Cardinal, Merry
del Val, the Cardinal-Secretary of State, I made still

closer acquaintance and one that had a curious sequel.
There was a charming young Don at Oxford, a friend
and fellow-Catholic of Urquhart, whom I will call 'Q'.
Knowing that 'Q' was to spend the vacation in Rome,
'Sligger' had kindly written to ask this elder man to
befriend me. In due course a note arrived from 'Q',
inviting me to meet Cardinal Merry del Val for a
private view of a newly discovered Catacomb, not yet
open to the public, that contained some very ancient
paintings. Here was an opportunity indeed. I was
interested in the Catacomb, and no less interested in
meeting a real, live Cardinal.

Cardinal Merry del Val was delightful. Not yet
forty, slim, good-looking, speaking English like an
Englishman, he greeted me most affably, and began at
once upon the subject of last summer's cricket season.
What had happened to Gloucestershire? I would have
given much at that moment to have been a dry-bob.
I minded acutely my inability to explain to a Cardinal-
Secretary of State what had gone wrong with Gloucestershire's batting — or was it their bowling? But no
harm was done, for he promptly explained it to me
instead. He was friendly, informal and chatty. He
told us that at the Conclave at which Pius X had been
elected Pope, his own duty had been to carry the
messages that passed between the Cardinals, immured
in their separate cells, while the week-long combina-
tions and cabals were formed and re-formed, and that
he had completely worn out a new pair of shoes while
hurrying up and down the long stone passages of the
Vatican. (He did not tell us that, in order that the
saintly peasant-Patriarch of Venice should, when Pius
X, have the little local Venetian newspaper he loved

laid before him each morning with his coffee, the printing-press had been transported bodily from Venice to the Vatican cellars, where the leading articles could be composed, and the foreign news carefully selected, under Merry del Val's own prudent and statesman-like eye. I learnt that later from the same Protestant source that had so spiced my passing glimpse of Cardinal Rampolla.)

I glanced down, involuntarily, for the worn shoes, but on this occasion the great man was wearing a very smart pair indeed, with silver buckles, and above them scarlet stockings under his black cassock. As he scrambled up and down the short ladders among the excavations, he held up his skirts and displayed these stockings up to the knee, and the more I saw of them, the more vividly it came home to me that here was I, an Oxford undergraduate, making a threesome with a Cardinal and a Don in a place that no member of the public had yet been allowed to enter. There was a kind of 'What do you think of that, old cock?' conversation, unspoken but none the less real for that, going on inside me; and although at the time I believed myself to have been genuinely excited by the vestiges of early Christianity shown to me with so much knowledge and enthusiasm by this Prince of the Church, the betraying fact remains that, while I have forgotten the treasures of that dark honeycomb, I have remembered the scarlet stockings. It is humiliating to discover oneself to have been, when young, in the Middle-West-woman-tourist class of traveller.

But it was after we had taken leave of the kindly Cardinal that an extraordinary incident occurred. On either side of the main exit from the newly opened tunnels lay heaps of bones, looking rather like the dumps of sugar-beet that cumber the verges of East Anglian roads in November. These pyramids of bones, roughly screened by the workmen from the waste of the new tunnellings, had every appearance of waiting for the contractors' rubbish carts to carry them away. Now my family had a friend, Katie Wingfield (the Miss 'A' of Frederic Myers and the Journals of the S.P.R. at the beginning of this century), who, in addition to her other remarkable powers as a medium, had the gift of what is known as 'psychometry'. On one occasion, for example, she was handed a brown paper parcel, the contents of which were unknown to her. Holding the parcel in her hand, she gazed into a crystal, and there saw a series of happenings which were evidently taking place in ancient Egypt, including the hauling of gigantic blocks of stone across a sandy waste towards a half-built pyramid, the blocks being slung between tall wooden cylindrical rollers, before which skins were laid down upon the sand, like carpets, by a horde of brown-skinned workmen. The parcel, when opened, turned out to have contained a mummied hawk, taken from an Egyptian tomb.

Remembering this, it occurred to me that it would be interesting to take home with me to England one of these bones and, concealing its identity and provenance, to ask Katie to 'psychometrise' it. She might, I thought, see interesting crystal-pictures of the early Roman Christians. Accordingly I picked up a small bone, about the size of my little finger, and put it in my pocket. Walking home with 'Q' I naïvely produced the bone and told him what I intended to do with it.

The effect was staggering. There, on a Roman

pavement, this gentle-mannered Don appeared, in a flash, to go raving mad. His sudden fury was dumb-founding. He heaped abuse upon me. He said that relying upon Urquhart's introduction, he had imagined that he had had to do with an English gentleman, not a cad. I had insulted the Cardinal and abused his hospitality. I had broken every rule of honour and decency. I had deliberately committed the deadly sin of sacrilege. I was an outsider, and a base one. His dark eyes flashed in his pale, handsome, but now dis-torted, face.

I was very much taken aback. I had no idea what it could all be about. When his rage was exhausted, I said that I was very sorry to have offended, but what had I done wrong ? Were not these bones going to be thrown away in any case ?

'Don't you realise,' he shouted, 'that for all we know that may be the bone of a Martyr, or even of a Saint ?'

The thought had not struck me. Even at this day I am ignorant of why a Martyr, already crowned in bliss, or a Saint, already eternally in the presence of God and capable of effectually interceding with Him on behalf of those still in the flesh, should require one of his or her smallest bones, no bigger than my little finger, to be left on or near the spot where it had been laid at his or her death. One would have thought that the re-assembly of the bodily skeleton on the Day of Resurrec-tion, so vividly described by Agrippa d'Aubigné, could have had but little importance to those already possessing the freedom of the Celestial City. But clearly, since 'Q' was not only a good Catholic but a man of the highest intelligence, one would be wrong so to think.

I could only renew my apologies, and assure him

I

that I had intended neither insult, betrayal of hospitality, nor sacrilege. Calming down, 'Q' told me to take the bone back and to lay it exactly where I had found it. He would wait for me.

I went back about a quarter of a mile. I could not remember the exact spot from which I had taken the bone, but recollecting that every particle of bodies eaten by lions or blown to smithereens by explosives will be neatly reassembled at the Resurrection, I did what the dog 'So-So' in Mrs. Ewing's story would have done, and threw it down 'there or thereabouts'. In any case I was now unobserved. 'Q' was waiting for me in the street, and I must say made handsome amends for his outburst. He had recognised, he said, that by showing him the bone I had proved my inno-cence of evil intentions, and that I must be acquitted on the score of my invincible ignorance. He withdrew 'cad' and all the rest of the abuse. We shook hands. I thanked him for my interesting afternoon. We met several times later at Oxford, and he was always amiable and kind to me.

But the scene left its mark. It was the third occasion in my experience upon which a mature and educated man had completely lost control of himself over an unwitting offence by myself against his God. The first time, as I have told elsewhere, was when I offended the God of an Anglican Rector (who thought it foolish to tell the truth when selling a horse) by leaving a handful of oats upon a Bible when I went to bed. The second God whose wrath I incurred was the God of a young Cambridge man preparing for Ordination. This God regarded the utterance of an obscene word by a small boy who had not the ghost of an idea what it meant as the depth of infamy. And now here was yet another God, the God of a delightful, cultivated Oxford Don, outraged at the further removal of a small bone which a Cardinal had already, through his workmen, roughly torn from its resting-place and thrown upon a heap with perfect nonchalance. In each case the devotee of the God concerned had made no attempt to find out my motive or whether there was any *mens rea*, as the lawyers say : he had instantly assumed my full guilt and felt it due to his Deity to fly into a passion. If I have dealt at undue length with this and the previous incidents, it is because I believe that they illustrate, in little, the causes of secular persecutions and wars of religion in which so-called Christians have permitted themselves to indulge. And since these three Gods — the Rector's, the Ordinand's and the Don's — would have been equally incomprehensible to Jesus of Nazareth, these three youthful experiences could only confirm me in my growing suspicion that institutional religion has nothing whatever to do with the Kingdom of Heaven.

When not church-hunting, we were inclined, as a family, to look for 'views', and must have driven some miles across the Campagna in pursuit of them, for I remember vividly a winter afternoon when the dome of St. Peter's rose solitary from the plain, like a mosque in Robert Byron's 'Oxiana', as if all Rome had been flattened by some catastrophe during our excursion, and only one shapely mound remained, the colour of an amethyst. And indeed the scale of that tremendous dish-cover can only be realised from far away : at hand it could conceivably be open to the criticism of the Second Workman on whom Lord Desborough once eavesdropped beneath the dome of St. Paul's :

First Workman : 'Bloody 'igh, ain't it, Bill ?'

Second Workman : 'Not so bloody.'

First Workman : 'Well I bet you never see a bloodier.'

There is a faint feeling of 'not so bloody' as one approaches the façade of St. Peter's across the great pool of sunshine flanked by those embracing colonnades ; but, seen from the Janiculum, it is already majestic, and from the Campagna one knows that the First Workman has it every time.

Nor did we, of course, neglect the painters and the statuary. My father had a great capacity for admiration, provided he was shown what to admire, and before paintings which had been awarded two or more asterisks by Baedeker he would stand for impressively long periods, with an expression of profound under-standing. He seemed to have no preferences as between artists of the first rank, and had the same reverential attitude towards the tortured twistings of the Laocoön as towards the still simplicity of a mourning figure on an archaic tomb. I was entranced by the mourner, and did not like the Laocoön, but I did not say so, for I could not then believe that the almost religious look in my father's expressive countenance could be called forth by anything less than perfect of its kind. And since with Michelangelo and Raphael and the rest of the three-star painters it is not easy to go wrong, it was a united family that cricked its neck in the Sistine Chapel and walked those cold Roman galleries. It was not until many years later that I discovered that, so far as architecture or painting was concerned, my father, with no human mentor or guide-book to direct him, was as helpless as the blind. It was not all loss for him, however, since it enabled him to live for the last thirty years of his life in an interior of singularly repellent aspect, not only without any twinge or prick of pain, but with unruffled acquiescence.

During my mother's life he had her always at his side to keep him straight about art, for her own father, whose spiritual home had been Italy, had been a member of the Arundel Society, and she had been brought up among those gallant reproductions which, with the limited technical resources then available, did so much, in an era of bad taste, to embellish the spare bedrooms of our country homes and the drawing-rooms of our Rectories. So that in Rome, and I think more especially among the Raphaels, and provided her grown-up son averted his eyes, as she averted hers, from the occasional nude goddesses, my mother was in her element, and I think the exhilaration of those weeks of keen frosty air and unbroken sunshine must have helped her to understand what had befallen her own father, in that rejuvenating climate, some years before. For James Johnstone Bevan, a lone widower, was already in his late seventies, bald, white-bearded and sinking into apathy and melancholy, when a curious thing happened to him. As he was being driven through the Suffolk lanes in his carriage, thinking dreary thoughts or none at all, something, as he afterwards described it, 'snapped' in his brain. He sat bolt upright ; he began to hum airs from the Italian operas he had once known so well. That night he wore a buttonhole at his solitary dinner ; he bade Norgate, his butler, bring a Continental Bradshaw ; he resolved to revisit Italy and his old haunts. In a matter of days Norgate found himself, pained and astonished, eating distasteful Italian food in Florence while his master, still humming and standing again his full six-foot-five in his smart new clothes, was 'doing' the galleries and the Churches with all the ardour of a young man. From Florence they went to Rome ; there was no watchful mamma to chaperone him among the flower-girls in the Piazza di Spagna, and in no time at all the brisk old gentleman was carrying their wares, cost what they might, to the hotel where Miss Alice Addington, thirty years his junior, was staying with her elderly father, Lord Sidmouth. He wooed and won her by a *coup de main*, and returned to England with a spirited stepmother, not much older than herself, for my mother and an indulgent 'Aunt Alice' for us children. But the air of Rome is one thing and that of Suffolk another, and my gay old grandfather's second youth did not endure. Another drive with his wife, and whatever had snapped un-snapped again ; he broke off in the middle of 'La Donna è mobile' to relapse, in a moment, into apathy and senectitude. It must have been some relief to his disillusioned bride when gaiety returned with second childhood. The last time I saw him he was sitting at the head of his dinner-table wearing a white tie, tail-coat and a pink carnation, and singing 'Oh, dear ! What can the matter be !' at the top of a still lusty voice, while banging his spoon on the table in time with the song.

The only painting — or rather fresco — of which I took home a reproduction to hang in my rooms at Balliol was Guido Reni's 'Aurora', a choice which probably reflects nearly enough my untutored taste at nineteen. I imagine my great-grandfather would have made much the same selection, unless he had picked a Carlo Dolce instead. But on a later vacation, when I joined my parents in Florence, I knew better. For, in

the meantime, there had been many an evening in
Cyril Bailey's rooms, spent in turning over our host's
collection of photographs of Renaissance paintings and
listening to a running commentary that took nothing
for granted, demanded no acquiescence, yet somehow
sharpened our powers of perception and comparison
while infecting us with Cyril's own enjoyment.
Besides, I had read my Berenson, and could look out
for 'tactile values' with a docile and obedient eye.
Botticelli held, I think, for my generation the position
that Piero holds today : he was the touchstone of a
good taste that none could call in question. For there
is a fashion in admiration, and one of the satisfactions
of growing older is no longer to follow fashion, either
in clothes or taste ; but to choose one's painters, as
one's clothes, for one's own comfort alone. And then
the giants no longer contend for supremacy, but each,
exciting or serene, gives what he, and he alone, has to
give.

A first look at Rome was, for me, a first look at the
Roman Catholic Church. I did not approach it in
complete ignorance, or with any prejudice, for in reading aloud, my father had been fond of offering us
passages from Newman for our admiration, and two of
my mother's favourite aunts were devout Catholics.
Indeed, there had been a miracle in the family, and one
which I cannot help feeling would have made a greater
stir if it had happened elsewhere than in Rutlandshire.
The miracle was this : one of my mother's favourite
aunts was married to Mr. Charles Eaton of Tolethorpe
Hall. 'Old Uncle Charlie' was not sympathetic to his
wife's creed or to her piety. When he was not making
fun of her punctual observance of every obligation of a

good Catholic, he was grumbling or growling because some of them could not be performed without the help of the carriage-horses. He could not see why the carriage-horses should risk their health because a Feast of the Church happened to coincide with the sort of weather from which sensible Protestants safeguard these valuable creatures. My great-aunt bore it all with patience, but, in secret, never ceased to pray for his conversion. And, at long last, her prayers were heard. For Great-uncle Charles, already elderly, was travelling up to London when, looking out from the train, he saw the Virgin Mary standing, surrounded by light, in the middle of a field of turnips. He was not the sort of man to contemplate the possibility that Our Lady might be appearing for some other passenger in the train, or even for some other purpose than to save the soul of Charles Eaton. He accepted the compliment, took the hint with a good grace, and was received into Mother Church. There was no more talk about the carriage-horses, who now turned out in all weathers to carry his wife and himself to their duties ; and he ended his days peacefully and kindly, telling his beads over the drawing-room fire. But neither church nor shrine was erected in the turnip field where the vision had been vouchsafed ; and there is no Blessed Eaton in the company of Bernadette. For the Roman Church has nothing if not tact ; and there are times and places when and where, and others when and where not, to make much of miracles. Rutlandshire in the nineties fell into the second category.

As the great-grand-nephew by marriage of a man whom nothing short of a miracle could have been enough to, and a miracle did, convert to the Faith, I had

already a tenuous link with Catholic Rome, and I could
not but be impressed by the fact that, having gone
thither with no other thought but to see the classic
remains, I had within a few days found myself entirely
engrossed in the wonders and splendours of the
Christian city. In all civilisations the finest works of
man have been religiously inspired, but no other religion
has approached the achievements of Christianity, in
scope, variety, beauty or magnificence. It makes no
difference that my father, after gazing at a Madonna
and Child by Fra Lippo Lippi, should have consulted a
guide-book, looked grave, whispered to my mother,
and caused her to turn pink as she gave to the exquisite,
fair-haired Lucrezia Buti a second scrutiny. A renegade
clerk painting his mistress as the Mother of God owed
as much to the Faith as Sandro himself when he
abandoned his pagan subjects at the bidding of Savon-
arola. The patrons, whether Lorenzos or Popes, may
have been unbelievers at heart, but tradition and the
inescapable beauty of the Gospel stories assured the
continuing pre-eminence of 'sacred' themes even
through the years of the new humanism. And the
painters and sculptors and modellers in faience had the
great piece of good fortune, that they knew, thanks to
Matthew and Luke, certain sacred mysteries of which
the earliest Christian writers, Paul and Mark, make no
mention. Nor does the author of the Fourth Gospel
refer to them. It is possible that Paul, whose writings
were nearest in time to the life of Jesus, and Mark, who
very probably made use of Peter's own memories, did
not know of the Nativity stories, but the author of the
Fourth Gospel must have known them, as we do,
through Matthew and Luke. Yet he rejected them,

strongly as they would have fortified his thesis of the
Logos incarnate. Moreover, even Luke repeats Mark's
story of how the people of Nazareth behaved to their
young Carpenter in a manner that would have been
incomprehensible had those stories of His birth been
true. On such slender foundations are based all the
exquisite Annunciations, Mothers and Children, Holy
Families, Nativities, Visits of the Magi and Flights into
Egypt that have made Christian art more human, more
moving and poetic than any other. To the simple-
hearted Catholic countries Luke and Matthew have
given, in despite of theology, a Woman Goddess to
petition and to adore, and to all of us, whatever our
creeds, an incomparable heritage of beauty. We owe
them much. Even Dr. C. J. Wright, not long ago
deprived of his teaching functions by his Archbishop
for pointing out to his pupils the tenuity of the evidence
of the Virgin Birth, must feel that the world, even if
misled, has been enriched by those legends.

My first look at the Roman Church, then, left me
with an impression of dignity, beauty and achievement.
I had enjoyed hob-nobbing with a Cardinal. I loved
the blue-robed, singing nuns. I sniffed incense with
relish. I was fascinated by the pageantry of High Mass.
I was in love with the architecture of the ages of Faith.
Only two things marred the picture for me : that scene
about the bone, and the Minor Canons in the choir of
St. Peter's. The Minor Canons worried me so much
that I consulted Urquhart about them on my return to
Balliol. He pouted, admitted that he had noticed what
I had noticed, but said that they were people of no
importance. What we had both noticed about the
Minor Canons, chanting in their stalls, was that they

had horrible faces. Each one might well have sat to a Mantegna for a portrait of Sloth, Gluttony or Lust. Their features were gross, greasy and sensual. Their chanting was heavenly ; but the ear's delight was paid for too dearly by the eye, and more dearly still by the offence to decency and decorum. I was deeply shocked, and only many years later read somewhere that the celebrated criminologist Lombroso once made an experiment. He mixed together a large collection of photographs, which included those of bishops, divines, statesmen, philosophers and philanthropists, with those of murderers, sadists, crooks and lechers. Having shuffled them well, he asked a number of experienced judges, doctors, psychologists and policemen to pick out the criminals. All failed : the number of exemplary characters selected was as great as that of the convicts. Had I known of this at the time it may be that the shock given to me by the Minor Canons of St. Peter's would have been much diminished. Those dreadful faces may well have been masking hearts of gold.

At nineteen I knew little history and less theology. Although already sceptical about sacramental and redemptive doctrines on moral grounds, I was still ignorant of the strength or weakness of their historical bases. Nor did I know anything of the history of the Roman Church in action. I was as unaware of the life of St. Francis as of the persecutions of the Jews in Spain. So I came away from that enchanting visit with, on the whole, a deep sense that Mother Church was a very high-born Lady indeed.

It must have been three years later that I joined my parents during the Long Vacation at Menaggio on Lake Como, for it was there that I received the not unexpected telegram from Hancock to tell me that I had only achieved a Second Class in Greats. But whatever my expectations, I doubt if the result of a mere examination could have damped my spirits in that delectable place.

We had been at Rome in winter when the days were short and the cold very sharp indeed, and economy had excluded us from that most engaging part of Italian life, the evening café. It is true that on one occasion we had been to a performance of *Julius Caesar* in Italian, in which Mark Antony, played by an enormously fat actor, ran his race in a gent's striped bathing-costume, and the back-cloth, with startling prescience, represented the Arch of Titus. But most of our evenings had been spent round a fire of green logs, in doing our 'prep' for the next day's culture-hunt, with Marion Crawford and Baedeker and Augustus Hare for text-books. We had done no lounging or sauntering, nor tasted the sun-drenched lizard-life that Italy demands. But here, at Menaggio, Italy was herself. The very first night I woke to hear fishermen, out upon the Lake, singing the 'Miserere' in true Italian voices, and looked out from my balcony to see their lateen-sails black in the white pathway of the moon. The scene could have been 'laid on', as the army would say, by some romantic impresario for my personal enchantment. The night was warm, and the tops of the mountains on the far side of the lake were faint and milky in the moonlight. Bellagio glimmered on like Tennyson's peacock. There was a plash of oars when the singing ceased, but otherwise everything was still. A scene to remember, and I have remembered it.

Olive and cypress, oleander and vine, mountain and

lake, little bursting black figs in the market at about twopence a pound, slender campaniles, shadowed arcades at noon, all the ingredients of Italian magic which has ever since held me spellbound, were there, at Menaggio, Bellagio, Varenna, Tremezzo, under a constant sky, in a dependable warmth. The hills behind the town, and those steeper ones that overhang Varenna, were naturally terraced with little lawns of fine grass, untroubled by dock or nettle, spread beneath Spanish chestnut trees. It is distracting to have to decide upon which of these lawns, where the light falls greenish through the long, bold chestnut leaves, to open the luncheon-basket. The next always looks better. The most united of families, the best of friends, get 'edgy' and tiresome over choosing the spot for a picnic. As the young man of the party who did most of the carrying I generally got my way : besides, I was right. But it is melancholy to reflect how vileness appears, in however infinitesimal a sample, not only where, but because, every prospect pleases.

But I was a professional wet-bob in those days, and did not often abandon the lake for the hills. All the same, it was not all pleasure when the news reached the Villa Trench that an Oxford Blue and his reverend cousin, a Magdalen and Leander oarsman, were staying at Signor Bullo's hotel. The Villa Trench, for all its green shutters, has an English look ; an uncompromising avenue of young cypresses, straight as a ruler, leads up to it from the high-road, and in it dwelt Mr. Trench, the King of Cadenabbia. Mr. Trench was elderly, authoritative and kind. He had the fruitiest voice in the world, and he used it less for conversation than command. A note from Mr. Trench summoned

Lumley Green-Wilkinson and myself to meet him at
the boat-house of the Villa Trench, where a four-oared
clinker-built boat with sliding seats was tethered. Mr.
Trench, sunburnt and white-haired, sat with an irre-
proachably straight back at the stroke thwart. I was
number three. Lumley and a fourth oarsman, whom
Mr. Trench's infallible nose and fruity voice had scented
and summoned, completed the crew. Mr. Trench
belonged to the stately school of strokes ; he liked to
paddle at about fifteen to the minute. The sun blazed
down ; we had no shorts, and the oil from the runners
fouled our white flannels ; we rowed down the lake
and we rowed up the lake ; our progress was sedate,
processional and joyless. When we at length landed,
Mr. Trench at his fruitiest told us how much we had
enjoyed it, how soon we must do it again. But he gave
us a very good tea.

The best means of Trench-dodging was to be already
on or in the lake when the fell summons arrived, but
it would be unfair to regard that hospitable enthusiast
as the frying-pan from which on one occasion we so
narrowly missed falling into the fire. Lake Como can
be at her calmest before a storm ; the brief hurricanes
which rush down upon her from the mountains to
fleck her surface with white horses and to dissolve her
still reflections of oleander and balustrade into angry
spray, give little or no warning of their sudden malice.
And it was not to dodge the four-oar, but to take
advantage of a windless afternoon that Lumley and
I picked out the lightest available pleasure-boat and
rowed across to Bellagio, steered by my elder sister.
Even our return journey was begun without misgivings,
but at about three-quarters of the way back we noticed

sudden clouds above Bellagio, and an ominous white
line upon the water far astern of us. Our boat was a
cranky affair with little or no freeboard, and we began
to row for our lives. The white line gained upon us
all the time ; it represented a wave like a miniature
'bore', not very high, but high enough to break over
and swamp us. My sister could not swim ; we rowed
as hard a finish as in any of our Henley races, and won
by about two boat-lengths, stepping ashore among a
crowd of yelling Italians. We ought to have known
better, because some years before, when an Eton boy,
I had shared with my family a much more alarming
experience near Tremezzo. The same sudden storm
fell on us from a serene sky ; but this time we had
young children with us, and as soon as the waves, all
but unannounced, began to slop over the gunwales, the
Italian boatman who, like Mr. Linklater's hero, had not
the *don di coraggio*, let go his oars, fell upon his knees
and prayed loudly to the Virgin and the saints. This
visual evidence of what the local expert thought of our
chance of survival was discouraging to the children ;
luckily my father, though never a wet-bob, could
handle an oar, and he and I managed to beach the boat
in a shingly cove. My father refused to pay the boatman, a gesture which must have seemed very harsh to
him, since his prayers had been heard and answered.
But we had a long walk home before us in the dusk,
partly through a tunnel which was even more terrifying
to my youngest sister than the storm, and, with all the
arrogance of the Protestant Englishman, felt that we,
and not the saints, had done the trick. I ought, as I
have said, to have remembered that earlier bolt from
the blue, and to have kept the one safe rule for Lake

Como, which is to use light boats only within easy reach of port.

The Rev. Lumley Green-Wilkinson, once famous at Magdalen as 'Grugger', must have been the merriest soul that ever wore a dog-collar. As holiday-chaplain to the Trench-ridden British colony, he took his solitary meals in a corner of the cool dining-room of the Hotel Victoria, but could not help twinkling at the English family which, he afterwards declared, broke all the rules of British behaviour by talking incessantly at table. Chaplains have their names on hotel notice-boards, beneath discreet little black crosses and a time-table of Sunday services, and my mother remembered a cousin who had married a General Green-Wilkinson. So, in an airy way that committed us to no church-going, she accosted the twinkler, and found that he was indeed the son of the General, who was solacing his old age by papering his spare rooms with postage-stamps. From that moment Lumley joined our table and our expeditions, and kept us in a state of almost unbroken merriment. When not on holiday he was private Chaplain and Secretary to the Archbishop of York, Cosmo Lang, with whom he eventually went to Lambeth as Controller. It was an improbable partnership of mutual devotion : Lumley cracked schoolboy jokes to the Archbishop, and the Archbishop reiterated, as the months and years and decades went by, 'Lumley, shall I never fathom your abysmal ignorance ?' He never did, but it could not signify, for so golden-hearted and unselfish a man as Lumley had no need of book-learning.

It was in Lumley's company that I discovered another streak of treachery in the character of that bewitching

Lake. We used to row out in a boat and dive over-
board for a swim. For the most part, the water was as
warm as water should be that has absorbed, for many
summer months, the rays of an Italian sun. But once
in a while a dive would be into water so icy as to be
terrifying. One rose to the surface numbed and scared
and breathless. There is no surface sign to give warning
of these sinister and Kelpie-like currents, and the shock
of a sudden encounter with their cold hostility, amid
such circumambient warmth, is most unpleasant. But
one bathe I shared with Lumley remains in my memory
as one of the most exciting experiences of my life. At
the close of a sultry day one of those sudden storms
broke over Menaggio itself. It was just before dinner,
and we ran from the hotel to take advantage of this rare
opportunity of swimming in big waves. Continuous
thunder was crashing overhead and echoing among the
mountains ; the lightning was incessant, and while
we were in the water an extraordinary blue light
shimmered and quivered, at surface level, all around us.
It was like bathing in summer lightning. I was quite
unscientific, and believed that the water made us immune
to any danger ; but the electrical discharge, or whatever it was that caused this phenomenon, had a most
stimulating physical effect. Every sense was enhanced ;
and the slapping waves, the darting lightning, the hissing
of the rain, the clamour of the thunder, and the blue
light that flickered all about us combined to make that
bathe, in point of sheer physical exhilaration, an unforgettable delight.

The pleasure to be got from scenery, and more
particularly from the sight of mountains, is not, it
seems, atavistic. Our forefathers had, throughout the

K

centuries, laid little store by it. They lived near the bone, and preferred a prospect of corn and vines and fruit-trees to that of rugged and desolate hills. It is a pleasure for the privileged, whose living is assured, to throw an admiring and not a mere calculating farmer's eye over a landscape. And one must be doubly privileged in order to reach the places where the scenery is displayed. So I must count myself fortunate, with a low bow to my parents, for having been given the chance of first tasting a pleasure which, of all others, seems least inclined to pall. Life at Balliol was exhilarating enough : to lead it against a vacation-backcloth of mountain and lake was richness indeed. And now that the more strenuous delights of deer-stalking and shooting and fishing are things of the past, it is a wonderful solace to be able to turn, with undiminished zest, to the sight of those high hills, receding in sunlight or advancing after rain, which first stirred me so long ago.

VII

IT has often been held that Oxford is the more humane of the two senior Universities ; that Cambridge, if not exactly cold-hearted, at any rate puts intelligence before feeling. But in one respect Oxford can claim to be the more intelligent as well as the kinder of the two, if common sense can be regarded as akin to intelligence. For at Oxford a freshman, on arrival, goes straight into College ; he is conducted by the under-porter across the Quad, or through narrow, ancient archways, or beneath arcades and cloisters, to a doorway where he finds his own name stencilled in white upon a square of glistening black paint, at the foot of a staircase. The window of his sitting-room looks out, as like as not, upon an enclosed or partly enclosed space : there may be lawns or gravel, or gardens, or trees, and in the enclosing walls, often of heart-lifting beauty, mostly venerable, and always, even when ugly, transfigurable by affection, are the stones of his own College. He is an inhabitant of his 'domus', snug inside the fold, and the men on his staircase will drop in to inspect him and, if he passes muster, to make him welcome. Even if he is too shy, too awkward, to be immediately assimilated by the little society in which he is enrolled, he has the best of chances, by propinquity, by shoulder-rubbing on the steps of Hall or before the notice-boards on the Porch, of turning familiarity into acquaintance, acquaintance into friendship. However shorn of social gifts the lamb, the wind is tempered to him by the enfolding College walls. By the time the Oxford man has to be turned out of College into 'digs', he has made his friends and his enemies, found his appropriate place in society, and can retire to Long Wall or to Beaumont Street warmed and reassured by at least two years of staircase companionships. He can choose his fellow-lodgers ; and, if he wants to work, he can do so undisturbed.

At Cambridge it is the other way about. The fresh-man begins life in remote and lonely 'digs' ; he visits, but does not inhabit, his College ; his face remains unfamiliar to his seniors ; and at night, the proper time for confidences and discoveries, his own College gates are implacably shut against him.

I was myself lucky enough to spend three years in College, and when at last the time came to move out, I made, together with Douglas Radcliffe and Eric Romilly, a mistake which has been, is being, and will be made so long as seventeenth-century small stone houses endure. There is something about the outward aspect of a little, gabled manor-house or vicarage with its roofs of weathered stone tiles, and small mullioned windows, that makes anyone with half an eye long to live inside it. We three had many times admired, and longed to live inside, the Old Parsonage in the Banbury Road. Our longing was misplaced. It is a mistake to work and to eat in a long, low room barely illumined by a single window with more stone than glass in it. It is a still greater mistake to sleep in a bedroom in which those coveted gables force your swinging looking-glass to bow uselessly towards you, that has no fireplace, and where the floor slopes so much that the water in your round tin bath collects in a pool by the rim, a pool too small to sit in. And the worst mistake of all, if you are more than six foot four inches high, is to inhabit a dwelling in which the doorway, staircase and passages were designed for our pygmy ancestors of the seventeenth century. We were hardened to the cold in our College bedrooms, but not to darkness and to bumps. If our landlady had not been a rare hand at cooking succulent lamb-chops, covered with brown bread-crumbs, we should have grumbled a good deal, with only ourselves to blame. As it was, our dinners and our pleasure in each other's company reconciled us to our discomforts. To this day, when I drive through the Cotswolds and contemplate those fascinating little houses which are the envy of all who have never lived in them, I am good natured enough to hope that their inhabitants also are being comforted by lamb-chops.

My last year, except for the rowing and coaching, was given over to work. I was being driven by 'Fluffy' Davis, encouraged by 'A. L.', and beginning to dream, as I have told, of All Souls. It was usual to devote two years to reading for the final Schools in Modern History, but having taken Greats at the end of my third year, I was contracting the work of two years into one. It was a case of avowed 'cramming'. Had I achieved All Souls there could be nothing to say against it. The prize, in cash as well as in prestige, would have been well worth the grind. But since I was destined for the Bar, a profession in which a University degree counts for nothing, I am not sure that, in the event, the gaining of a First Class was sufficient justification for the pressure I was under. Nobody ought to write feverish essays in his sleep for weeks and months on end. And learning got by cramming is soon forgotten. I took as 'Special Subject' the Crusades. I received 'alpha plus' for my papers in that subject, and was congratulated by the examiners. Within a couple of years of going down, all that I knew of the Crusades were a few vague memories of *The Talisman*, which I read as a child. And when I began, in London, to read for the Bar, I found myself listless and lazy, and quite content to scrape through the examinations anyhow. Even a single year of over-working is dearly paid for by two years of mental apathy. I dwell on this experience, not because it is of any interest in itself, but because it raises, and illustrates, a difficult problem of University education. The end of such an education ought to be, I suppose, the enlargement of a young man's, or young woman's, capacity for acquiring wisdom, wisdom being defined as a sense of values, or the ability to choose between those things that are worth while and those that are not. To make such a choice needs a trained intelligence, to save its owner from being bamboozled ; a trained conscience, to keep his behaviour on the rails ; a trained heart, to teach his head to know its place and its limitations ; and trained powers of enjoyment, which perhaps are the most important of all, since when people are enjoying themselves they seldom get into mischief. This is a pretty large order to be handed down by the Dons in a space of three or four years, but, had it not been for Schools, I should not have put it past the capacity of the men, already described, who sat round the table in our Senior Common Room.

Is it conceivable that Davis should have said to me :
'You had better take the Crusades as Special Subject :
it is much the shortest', but for the necessities of Schools ?
Had I been handed over to him to be taught wisdom,
not to be hustled into a First Class, should I not have
been studying the New Enjoyment in the Fifteenth
Century, or the Decline and Fall of Superstition in the
Eighteenth rather than the *Gesta Francorum* ?

There was a general agreement at Oxford fifty years
ago, when economic pressure on young men was far
less severe than today, that the choice of studies and
Schools should not be governed by a man's destined
profession. The fact that I was going to spend my life
practising Law was accepted by all concerned as a valid
reason for my not reading Law at Oxford. The end
of education was conceived of very much as I have
stated it ; but I cannot help thinking that the Final
Schools, as far as we who tried for Honours were concerned, stood in the way of that end being achieved.
And nowadays, when a man must, if possible, earn his
living from the day he goes down, even the true end
has often to be relinquished. It is pleasant to speculate
about a far-off future when, common sense about procreation having reduced the population and applied
science having ensured leisure for us all, a University
will grant degrees, without examination, in Wisdom.
The subjects to be studied will not greatly differ from
those taught today. Intelligence will be trained, as
now, through Logic and Philosophy. It will exercise
itself upon History, with the same nice regard to
sources and evidence. The powers of enjoyment will
be enlarged through literature, ancient and modern,
through archaeology, through architecture, through

painting and music. Natural history, and such science as he can take, will at least be dangled, invitingly, before a young man's eyes. The training of the conscience can be done only by example ; but so long as Oxford can reproduce Strachan-Davidsons and A. L. Smiths, Urquharts and Baileys, a Hartley or a Davis, consciences will do well enough.

The training of the heart will be a more complicated affair : it was neglected in my day. We did not so much as notice that our servants, always about and among us, lived in basements by day and in attics by night ; that on their very holidays they wore drab, funereal clothes. But then the Dons did not notice it either. Of the anxieties and deprivation, the nagging insecurity of the majority of our countrymen, only one in twenty of us, if that, had sufficient awareness to be uneasy. Yet how can a young man expect to take his B.W. (Bachelor of Wisdom) degree if he fails, or only gets a 'gamma', in Compassion ? For when I say that there will be no examinations, I am speaking only of Final Schools. The degree of Bachelor of Wisdom will be awarded, not by a Board of strange examiners, but by the consensus of the Fellows of the candidate's own College, men who have summered him and wintered him and observed, not only his intelligence, but his morals and manners. The examination will be continuous, of the kind to which we subjected one another, less consciously and with smaller understanding, throughout our days and nights. And the fact that there will be no class-lists or order of merit will diminish the temptation, to which even Dons might succumb, of seeing that the New College dogs do not get the best of it. But this is fanciful, and being common sense as well, is never likely to happen. So I must return to my muttons.

It would be ungrateful in one whom a generous father kept for four years at Balliol, and to whom the Balliol Dons gave his full share of their unselfish hearts as well as of their distinguished minds, not to attempt to assess, in spite of the many imponderables, the extent of his debt to his College, as well as to the University at large. And I shall not speak here of the enduring comfort and refreshment of being able to call up, at will, memories of sheer happiness, nor of the friendships which, until the first Great War, multiplied occasions for delight, and have since, though cruelly fewer, buttressed from the outer side the walls that enclose my private felicity. It is of the profits of a Balliol education that I am thinking, the practical, day-to-day benefits of all that hard reading, enforced thinking, and disciplined living.

Such little learning, philosophical or historical, as I managed to acquire soon faded. But I feel sure that my intelligence was sharpened, by that obligatory practice, into a pretty serviceable instrument of general utility. I was, in the event, enabled to earn my living in a profession for which I had no natural aptitude and with which I had no traditional ties, family or social. Reading for Greats can have some unexpected results. Let me take a few instances. I have always had a dislike of machinery, and believed myself incapable of understanding how things work. When my father bought his first and last motor-car, he asked me to attend a course in London in order that one member of the family might know what went on under the bonnet. I protested that it would be useless, but he insisted. Cars were, in those days, simple enough, but the course was to last a week. At the end of the first two hours I, alone of the class, understood the beastly thing. Bradley's *Logic*, or some other such stiff book, had made the apprehension of the sequence of effects that follow an explosion in a cylinder mere child's play. The same thing happened in 1914. I was sent on a week's course to learn the mechanism of the Vickers gun. I was the only member of the class who had read Greats. On the third morning I was taken from the class to be an assistant instructor. In the City, where the most useful endowment is a nose for profits, which I lack, Greats again stood me in good stead. For, next to money-making, it is important, in affairs, not to lose money, for yourself or for your clients. And money is generally lost through losing sight of certain essentials ; by being bamboozled, that is, not necessarily by persons, but by the cloud of figures, opinions, hopes, market movements and estimates which envelop and often bedevil a business proposition. Now if Greats has not trained a man to pick out essentials, to separate the relevant from the irrelevant, nothing will. I still remember my almost comic despair when a group of senior business men, of great ability, but no University education, lost, not money, but untold time in discussing, over months and indeed years, a major scheme which, by reason of one simple fact that they had failed to grasp, never could have been practicable. I saw it and said it, as any other person with a Second Class in Greats would have seen and said it, at the first meeting, but was too junior to be listened to. Conference after conference took place ; extra chairs were carried in by the Commissionaire ; the telephone-lady was told that there must be no interruption ; newly created Knights, understood to know the mind of No. 10 Downing Street, sat on the corner of the leather sofa, their features expressing mystery and importance ; there were hints that the Governor of the Bank of England might not be indifferent ; flies had been thrown over powerful insurance companies ; the atmosphere was solemn and august. But I could not help noticing that the business was invariably referred to as 'the set-up' or 'the picture', and that it was a picture of the modern, not to say the abstract, school, wholly lacking precision. For what these distinguished men of business were trying to do was to found 'a Bank' which should finance a new industry on true banking terms, that is to say, by making well-secured advances at a moderate rate of interest.

It was a most laudable ambition, but what they had overlooked was that the products of the industry in question were to be Works of Art, and that no work of art (with the possible exception of paintings of Cardinals in red robes eating lobsters) can, while in process of creation, constitute a security in the banking or any other sense. The making of films is not only costly but in the highest degree speculative. Naturally the long-drawn-out talks came to nothing ; but they need never have been held had the talkers been given, by early training, an eye for essentials.

The point of these anecdotes is, of course, that an academic education does not, as is sometimes thought, unfit a man to earn his living. On the contrary, by sharpening his wit it can enable one with little Scottish and no Jewish blood in his veins to maintain himself even in the City. And I have little doubt but that if I had persevered at the Bar, my first choice of profession, I could, thanks to Balliol, have lived by it. There are principles, however thickly overlaid, behind the verbiage and intricacies of the law, and where there are principles a Greats man can usually, like a truffle-dog after truffles, nose them out.

So much for saying Grace after meat, or at any rate after bread-and-butter. Eating and drinking, at my own table and in company that never palls, has given to me, I suppose, more pleasure, quantitatively speaking, than anything else in life. For sheer quality of enjoyment I must put first such out-door pursuits as deer-stalking, or indeed any form of sport ennobled by high, presiding hills. The response to these rare delights is instinctive and partly physical; it would be absurd to thank the Balliol Dons for the ecstasies I have felt on Ben Heskernich or Misty Corrie. But there is a range of pleasures between these two extremes, a vast field of enjoyment into which Balliol turned me loose with, I feel sure, a better nose than could have been mine had I stepped straight from school into those same grazing-grounds. How far sensibility itself can be heightened by education, if at all, it is hard to say; but in enjoyment, as in the practical business of making a living, discrimination, the capacity not to be bamboozled, is all-important. The Dons taught us at least how to ring the coin. In reading, in picture-gazing, in the shaping of friendship out of acquaintance, in resistance to accepted ideas, in the defiance of slogans or superstitions, in the use of leisure, the capacity to reject is no less serviceable than the capacity to select. 'Skipping' is a valuable art, in living as well as in reading the Waverley Novels. I doubt whether many of my generation who sat of nights in Cyril Bailey's easy-chairs or on 'Sligger's' sofa, or by day in that comfortless ground-floor room where 'A. L.' stood behind the table with the check tablecloth, or who drank tea with Strachan or coffee with Warde Fowler, have been easily taken in by the pretentious or the second-rate. And if one is safe from that, well, it is much to be thankful for. Selection is another matter ; there is enough of the first-rate available to supply every man in his humour ; and it would be claiming too much to assert that Dr. G. M. Young is my favourite writer because he, too, once strolled about the Balliol Quad. The most I can say is, that had I not strolled there, I might well have missed the wriggling satisfaction of encountering a mind and a prose each worthy of the other.

I have been talking about training in the art of enjoyment, and the answer will be made that a great number of people enjoy themselves just as heartily with the second-rate, and, in any case, who is to be the judge of 'quality' ? That question has never been answered, and has become a bigger poser than ever before, now that every accepted standard in literature, painting and music, as well as in morals, is being hotly disputed. I can only say that I am thankful, none the less, for the kind of nose that Balliol gave me. The delights I have managed to sniff out with it, although admittedly the scents of a very small, walled garden, diminutive in time as well as in space, have tasted very good to me. And I am obstinately persuaded, although I can give no reasons for my persuasion, that had my nose received no training, I might have confused perfumes with smells.

There is, however, a much more serious objection to all this Oxonian complacency. 'The mistake you make', I have sometimes been told, 'is to make so much of happiness ; we were not sent into this world to be happy.' To those who have taken this line with me, my stressing of mere enjoyment will appear still less commendable. 'Did your good father', they will ask, 'spend all that money, and you yourself all those years, to sharpen your powers of enjoyment ? What about Duty, and Service, and Moral Purpose ?' Well, I have already admitted that the training of our hearts was inadequate, while claiming that our consciences could hardly fail to grow more tender in the light shed by those Dons of ours. As for Duty, very many of my generation died in its performance, and the rest of us were 'near misses'. And as for Moral Purpose, it is dangerously akin to Religion in one kind of person, and to what is nowadays called Ideology in another kind. Both are great begetters of wars and hatreds and conflicts of all sorts.

Happiness depends upon good fortune and temperament, and can hardly be the concern of a college or university ; but enjoyment can, it seems to me, be inculcated, and it is a major moral antiseptic. How harmless, friendly and civilised we are when enjoying ourselves ! In spite of the moralists, I shall continue to believe that to enlarge the field of enjoyment is a worthy end of education, and zest a part of wisdom.

It is not easy for a man who has turned his privileges to so small account and done little with his life except to enjoy it, to praise and to justify all the vast expense and devotion that went to his education. There are imponderables, of course, that defy description, and a system is entitled to be judged by its brighter as well as by its dimmer products. The stars of my generation were for the most part extinguished in the first Great War ; had they survived, I do not think it would have occurred to me, as it occurs to me now in this attempt to sum up what Balliol did for me, that it was yet another case of a sledge-hammer being employed to crack a nut. And some sledge-hammer !

That there were gaps in our schooling is undeniable. Although there was a Balliol Boys' Club in the Oxford slums to exercise us in practical compassion, most of us were content with admiring the unselfish few who ran it. Not that unselfishness, even when combined with compassion, is sufficient to make a successful club-manager. There must also be the capacity to remain unabashed in the presence of the boys, and to retain a certainty that there is greater need for the privileged to run a Boys' Club in the slums than for the boys to run a Man's Club among the privileged. When in later years I spent my Wednesday evenings at the Balliol Club in Hammersmith, I often felt hampered and embarrassed by the feeling that these gay and self-sufficient youngsters should have been giving up one night a week for work among young barristers. They could have taught us a good deal.

But I do think our political studies were maintained on too abstract a plane, and too seldom illustrated or tested by contemporary pressures and conflicts. I think we could have been turned loose from Balliol with a little more knowledge of the world, or at least of our own countrymen, than in fact we possessed. Un-worldliness is a chief desideratum for the will, but a danger for the mind. Another surprising gap, in a

Christian University and a College that made Chapel
compulsory on Sundays, was our lack of guidance to
some knowledge of the origins of a faith wholly based
on certain events in history. We were taught, in the
History Schools, to consult and to scrutinise original
sources, whether documents, inscriptions or other
evidence laid bare by the spade, but of the Christian
documents, for all that they are few enough, we were
taught nothing. Schweitzer's *Von Reimarus zu Wrede*,
a summary of more than a hundred years' work on the
New Testament by German scholars, appeared during
my second year at Balliol, and was not available in an
English translation until four years later, but we were
never so much as 'alerted' for this tremendous peace-
time raid from across the German Ocean. A study of
the probable dates, priorities, authorship and original
purposes of the New Testament documents, in their
setting of contemporary Jewish thought and speculation,
is bound to lead to a view of Christianity very different
from that so painfully compounded for us by the
warring theologians of the first four centuries. But
Balliol is not a seminary for ordinands, and it is curious
that a College with a tradition of following an argument
whither it might lead, regardless of consequences, was
so indifferent to the mighty issues of Christian truth.
I suppose that the Fellows believed in letting sleeping
dogmas lie, in view of the snarling and fighting apt to
ensue when they are aroused. But to one of our years
who has since been much preoccupied with Belief, it
seems odd that we should have been given neither
impetus nor the barest technical help towards the study
of the evidence for what was, if true, the most
stupendous event since life appeared on this planet.

Fifty years ago, had the schools and universities combined, in that St. Luke's summer of reason, to rescue the historic Jesus from the dying Creeds, his prescriptions for a sick world might have been taken more seriously by our leaders of thought and action. But we did not then think of the world as sick, and today, between the Anglo-Catholics on the one hand and the Billy Grahams on the other, the people go their busy ways with a shrug, and with no inkling of the Kingdom within them. As it was, I went down from Oxford no better instructed in these high matters than I went up, and have always had to do my own digging for 'origins'. There were continuous arguings, of course, mostly with Douglas Radcliffe, and the perennial human preoccupation with private 'God-making' was never laid aside for long. But the existence of God as a Person (and, curiously, as a male) was always taken for granted. We were concerned with His attributes, not His existence. And what some of us rejected in the Orthodox Creeds was rejected on moral, not on historical, grounds.

Although I am in no position, as an individual, to make out a case for all that devoted apparatus for enlightenment which is Oxford, there is one aspect of my personal experience which, in retrospect, leaves me uneasy. We were a family of six, two girls and four boys. Resources available for education were limited. My father had no hesitation in spending a wholly disproportionate amount upon myself. In a country where 'the first of the litter' counts even in the Constitution, it was not surprising that my father gave a lion's share to his eldest surviving son. But it ought to have been surprising. My next brother, destined from early days and by his own choice for the Navy,

L

cost little to educate, and had to live on his pay all his life. My youngest brother, too delicate for school, went to St. Andrews and eventually to Cambridge, but with no margin to buy, from time to time, a little jam to spread upon his bread and butter. Curates expect penury, and he was not disappointed. But next to nothing was ever spent upon the two girls. They were neither educated to support themselves nor given opportunities of meeting young men who might have worked to support them. Wandering about the Continent with their parents, or for brief spells living in temporary London quarters too narrow for entertaining, untaught even to dance, let alone to acquire social ease and self-confidence, they had to find within the cramping nutshell of family affection compensation for all the liveliness and adventure of that Edwardian world. The boys went to Balls ; the girls stayed at home ; and if a brother brought his men-friends to that home (or rather to those furnished lodgings in Harley Street or flats in Carlyle Mansions which sheltered the homeless) the girls had neither the clothes nor the confidence to profit from such casual contacts. During my mother's life, the daily exchanges of demonstrative affection between the members of this wandering quartet concealed from parents and daughters alike the true measure of the children's deprivations. At her premature death, which shattered at a blow the protective screen of her loving and untiring concern, they were left defenceless. They had been given no keys to unlock the doors of living, shown no finger-posts to self-reliance, and having submitted, with adoration, to her unconscious demands for unconditional surrender, were now waifs indeed.

At the time, we all took this state of unbalance for granted. 'Equality of opportunity' was not yet a political, far less a domestic, slogan. Thousands of other families were economising on the girls to send one bright boy to College. But, in looking back across fifty years, my gratitude for all that was lavished upon myself is a little clouded by the reflection that generosity rather than justice went to the shaping of my good fortune. And had I been one of my sisters, I should, I think, have felt the unfairness of it. To have been wholly untrained for the world would have seemed to me a high price to pay for being kept unspotted by it. And I should have wondered whether a little more management and forethought might not have resulted in some friends, some clothes, some continuous studies, less social diffidence, possibly some purpose or ambition. Perhaps my sisters did so feel and wonder. If so, they kept it to themselves. I do not think my father, who survived my mother by forty-three years, ever had a qualm or a regret. To him, daughters had their own place in the scheme of things, and an elder son had his. I cannot even be sure that, having watched that son for nearly seventy years, it ever occurred to him that there was little enough to show for so relatively massive an investment in a single one of five children living when it was made. Habitually open to fresh ideas, upon the relative importance of boys and girls, as on primogeniture, my father's mind was constant to the last.

But I was in my fourth year at Oxford, and living in the Old Parsonage, when I paused to stand back, and try to guess to what it all amounted, this enjoyable, expensive, leisurely education of mine. It is time to return to the Edwardian sunshine, before I lose my nerve in a sudden, chilling apprehension of the Parable of the Talents.

For all our absorption in work and games, our primary concern was with personal relationships. I am not sure that a profound, if secret, diffidence is not the most widely shared characteristic of young Englishmen. We learned to be afraid of one another at school ; as much afraid of showing affection as of failing to inspire it. The surest way of uncovering the hidden roots of diffidence in any particular person is to ask him what and whom he envies. For myself, I can recollect envying John Gore, of Trinity. I envied him in the first place for his face. However much I tried to be above such nonsense, I could never quite settle down with my own well-rounded countenance. I had mildly resented it even as a schoolboy, and now that my young man's fancy was beginning to take the Tennysonian turn, I began to regard it as a possibly serious handicap in the approaching quest for romance. A man's cheeks, I held and still hold, should be, if not actually furrowed as in Julius Caesar's case, yet never convex ; the bones of his nose, chin and jaw should be strongly marked. John Gore had a long, firm face, with none of the plump convexities which, I felt assured, young women must despise. But in addition to his clean-cut features — would *argutus* have been the Latin for his appearance ? — John Gore had social ease in the highest degree. He appeared to have friends in every College ; without athletic distinction, he did everything well, hitting a ball at any game as easily as he was reputed to hit a grouse ; he was amusing and amused ; he 'strove with none', had exceptional literary taste and knowledge for his age, and wore an air of ripeness and detachment from our own less mature preoccupations. I am not saying that I envied none but John Gore ; I would have given much for Alec Cadogan's poise and humour, and for this or that faculty or virtue in a dozen of my friends ; but I think John Gore's case best illustrates the kind of misgivings which beset me in everyday relationships with other men, and, on occasions, with young women. Nobody could ever have introduced John Gore, as they sometimes introduced me, as 'the rudest man in Oxford' ; I did not like it, and the fact that I never then understood the reason for this label goes far to explain how I came to earn it.

> Car c'est un petit fou qui se croit tout permis,
> Et qui pour un bon mot va perdre vingt amis.

If a *bon mot* came into my head, never mind at whose expense, I naïvely imagined that the object of it would be as much amused as I was. He rarely was ; and I was curiously slow to discover why I so often seemed to be more fond of my friends than they were fond of me. I suspect that we all lived by the affections to a far greater extent than we cared to acknowledge, and that I am not alone in thinking that our principal heartaches were caused not by failure in our athletic or academic ambitions, but by our own or others' shortcomings in the delicate art of friendship. As far as faces go, Sir Winston Churchill has removed once and for all any necessity for young Englishmen to suffer from curves or to pine for furrows ; but whether the present generation manages its friendships with fewer heart-burnings I do not know. The present is said to be an uninhibited age. In what way does exposure to light affect the mysterious motions of amity ?

One thing that the present generation of Oxford men will not easily understand is how woman-free were our lives. I do not mean that we had no day-dreams ; I had my own aching fantasies, absurdly incongruous with the real and the practical, and Rostand's 'La Princesse Lointaine' was, for me, not so much a romantic poem as a handbook. But we had no truck with girls in our courts and quadrangles and would certainly have regarded their daily and casual invasion of these sanctuaries as an interruption and a bore. Let them come, less as fellow-creatures than as a distant species, lightly touched by mystery, to Eights Week or to Commemoration Balls, but never to disturb our brave masculine preoccupations ! And when they did come, our relations with them were strangely formal and mannered. We waltzed with them at the Balls and they were in our arms, but for the thoughts and words we exchanged with them it was still the age of the square-dance and the minuet. There were pre-scribed reticences, and distances to be kept ; approaches and withdrawals were made to the beat of a traditional and accepted measure. Chaperones sat close at hand, veiling from us and our partners alike the experience in their eyes. Only at supper did the chaperones, but not the girls, admit to shared appetites. Our commerce with these guarded young persons could be enjoyable, or tantalising, or boring, but it was always circumspect. They could have had no suspicion of how we talked or thought or aspired among ourselves, and with us curiosity lingered to an age when the youth of the Continent were connoisseurs of women to a man. I remember, in this regard, a small dinner-party with 'A. P.', an Oxford doctor who coached the Magdalen

boat and took a kindly interest in all rowing-men. It
was a party of undergraduates, and over the port one
of our number boldly asked 'A. P.' whether women
enjoyed sexual intercourse. 'Speaking as a doctor,' said
'A. P.', 'I can tell you that nine out of ten women are
indifferent to or actively dislike it ; the tenth, who
enjoys it, will always be a harlot.' We accepted this,
from such an authority, as gospel. It is hard to imagine
a more mischievous message to young men, or one
more calculated to worry and to disconcert them. It
at once reproached all ardent bridegrooms and slandered
all willing brides. 'A. P.' was the kindest of men, and
the most honest ; and it is a measure of the false shame
demanded of his women-patients by the conventions of
fifty years ago that a doctor could be so ignorant. At
the time, my private reveries were too romantic and
ethereal for 'A. P.'s' words to have much significance
for me, but when I came to earth again I should have
been better off without the burden of them.

Personally I had little to do with Commemoration
Balls, since the tickets were expensive and dancing no
pleasure to me, for I had not yet been taught by Marion
Best, at a Dorsetshire dance, to forget my feet and to
obey the music with my shoulders, a 'tip' which made
me free, in a matter of minutes, of a keen and life-long
enjoyment. But on one occasion 'Commem.' caused
me no little embarrassment. I received a letter from
an American woman-friend of my parents asking me
to secure tickets for several College Balls for herself
and her two daughters, and to be their escort. I knew
her as a person of humour combined with that brand
of high-mindedness, continuously expounded, which is
peculiar to American ladies. She had shown much

hospitality to members of my family, and honour demanded that I should do my best for her in return. I was to entertain them once in my rooms in College, and to procure suitable young men for dinners at the Randolph and partners at the balls. I was sorry that the girls were not pretty, and that, in those powderless days, their noses were shiny ; but they were delightful, eager, natural young women, and I had no anxieties on their score. With time and trouble I was able to press into their service some of the more good-natured and less socially involved of my friends.

The festivities began with luncheon in my rooms. All went well ; Mrs. N. was gracious and high-minded as ever, and afterwards declared that Daniel Macmillan, the only guest whose name I remember, was a 'lamb'. But the dinner at the Randolph was not so successful. Our hostess was moody and distraite, and unduly formal with the men I had produced. I do not re-member if it was that evening or the next that the increasingly heavy atmosphere broke into thunder. But break it did, to my utter astonishment. Mrs. N. took me aside, and asked me whether it was because they were Americans that I had not introduced her girls to my aristocratic friends. It turned out that beneath all the humours and high-mindedness she was a howling snob. She had seen, painted in white letters at the foot of my own or other staircases in College, the names of what she called 'honourables' ; indeed there was even an Earl (by courtesy). Why did none of the partners I had procured have titles ? Where was that Oil ? This sudden descent of one who had introduced my family to *Wolfville* and *Rudder Grange*, and had needs must love the highest when she saw it, staggered me.

I cannot remember how I reacted to the shock. I think I must have asked if the girls, who were obviously enjoying themselves, shared her disillusion, for I was enjoined not to mention her complaints to them. Perhaps my dismay sobered her. I am sure she thanked me nicely when they left Oxford. But it was a jar to my young faith in human nature to discover that her pursuit of the highest included the pursuit, even at Oxford, of the highest in rank.

Although I am old-fashioned enough to believe that there was much to be said for our girl-free lives, and that we had fretting enough in our masculine friendships without the added distractions of summer frocks beneath the trees, I am no defender of the 'romantic' view of young women which was fostered, and preserved, by our normal separation from these fellow-creatures. No one can ever have fallen more deeply into the romantic heresy than I. Whatever in poetry or literature exalted and rarefied 'Woman' was embodied in my private canon of sacred writings. It led me for a couple of years into a fantastic by-way which cost me dear. It is a heresy which gives to its followers moments of ecstasy; but they must be paid for by disillusion. There have been few changes in the last half-century more sweeping than the rooting-out of this false doctrine. The wonder is how we who were deluded by it could ever have fallen into such error. For even when our reveries of some fugitive and unapproachable She, all loveliness and grace, were most continuous, we were perfectly aware of her extreme rarity. Our sisters, cousins, aunts and acquaintances, the maids, the women in the shops and streets were undoubtedly feminine, but none of them were 'Woman', not by a very long chalk. It was hard on them to be everlastingly disqualified by familiarity from becoming a wonder and a wild desire. It was the same with the fat, the plain, the spectacled. There were no hopes of being 'Woman' for them. Today, when Cape Turk has been rounded at last, and young men and girls mix on easy and companionable terms, the girls are known to be fellow-creatures after all. What is lost in day-dreaming is made up for by warmth and intimacy and the sharing of interests. There is still mystery enough for provocation ; still agreeable disturbance in the fall of a curl, or disquiet from the hang of a skirt, for sex sees to that ; but the days of formal and chaperoned reconnaissances are over, arm's-length has become arm-in-arm, and intelligence and charm and dearness come on the first encounter, not haltingly and in despite of looks, into their own. It is a great improvement.

There is no drama about going down from Oxford. Although Schools are over, the lists will not be published until the Vacation, and Oxford must be revisited for the 'Viva'. There are no formal good-byes ; a man's friends share his departure ; the Dons will be there, like the lamps and hearths of home, to warm and illuminate his many returns ; he may have, as I did, the secret pride of a Balliol man to sustain him, and the world is his oyster.

VIII

WHEN, owing to my inability to give any but the vaguest opinion upon some point of law, my friends throw doubt upon my assertion that I once upon a time practised as a barrister, I silence them with the remark that I have defended a murderer. It is true that he was hanged. But his was a difficult case to defend, since he wanted to be hanged. It was only because the Judge refused to accept his plea of 'Guilty' that I was asked by the Court, for a fee of two guineas, to undertake his defence. He had none. He was a jolly young sailor, who returned from a long voyage to find the girl he loved, and to whom he was betrothed, with a baby by another man. He cut her throat with a razor as she came down some stairs to meet him ; then gave himself up saying : 'I done it.' He was confident that, after the hanging, he would rejoin her in a better world. His was a happy, peaceful face. He gained a stone in weight awaiting trial in Maidstone Gaol. The Prison Governor warned me that I must not interview my client since he would tell me that he was guilty, and that I must not put him into the box since he would tell the jury the same. There was nothing I could do but extract from the doctor who examined the corpse an admission that the razor-wound could as well have been inflicted by the girl herself, and that it was not on the side he would have expected it to be, had it been made by a right-handed man facing his victim. I told the jury that nobody was there to see what happened ; and that if there was a scintilla of doubt, the accused man must have the benefit of it. The jury listened, as I thought, sympathetically. They glanced at the prisoner in the dock, whose eyes had the calmness of innocence, for all that he knew what the verdict would be. But the Judge put the jury to rights. 'Counsel told you', he said to the jurymen, 'that nobody saw what happened. That was incorrect. The prisoner was there, and he could have told you what happened. But he has not told you.' That, of course, was the end. They hanged my client, and he was glad to be hanged ; but I took it much to heart at the time, not because I had failed to do the impossible, but because I believed that sailor to have been of the loving and faithful sort. I forgot to reflect that, in his own view of the matter, he had escaped punishment altogether. I rather think that today he would have been reprieved ; it would have broken his heart.

Maidstone, where my client was hanged, is a principal Assize town on the South-Eastern or 'Home' Circuit, to which I belonged. Going on circuit was always a pleasant jaunt. There was a holiday feeling about wearing a bowler instead of a top-hat, and travelling first class, with a blue bag, containing wig and gown, in the rack. I do not think I had ever been in a first-class carriage before I was called to the Bar, but it was considered beneath the dignity of a barrister to travel second or third. I sank back into my unaccustomed seat, broad, yielding, and separated by an arm-rest from my neighbours, with a clear conscience. There are few minor satisfactions so complete as that of enjoying compulsory luxury.

We barristers stayed at a comfortable old Georgian Inn at Maidstone, and dined together in the evenings at a long table. We drank champagne and vintage port that cost us nothing, for our predecessors had lovingly laid down a cellar with the subscriptions of many years. Mr. Smither, the Circuit Butler, looked after us ; he was a handsome man of great courtesy and dignity, apt to be mistaken by young barristers for the Assize Judge. It was no surprise to learn that he was the father of Miss Denise Orme, a lovely young musical-comedy star who married Lord Churston. One of my fellow-beginners was a barrister of riper years ; he had been Attorney-General, or maybe a Judge, in a far-flung British Colony, and on retirement had joined one of the Inns of Court. We noticed that this kindly, sun-stained elderly man refused the champagne and the port, and bought himself a modest whisky-and-soda. About a year later he asked how it was that we briefless young men could afford such expensive wines. When told that the wines cost us nothing, the poor man nearly had a heart attack, and was never quite his cheerful self again. He seemed to be brooding over his lost, his irrecoverable opportunities. Barristers are the best of good company, for legal jests never pall, and Judges, as seen by the Bar, are infinitely diverting. Occasionally our mess was enlivened by Theo Mathew, the author of *Forensic Fables* and outstanding wit of the day, and there was competition to sit next to Mathew in the yellowish, varnished seats of Maidstone Court in order to overlook his brilliant sketches of Judge, witnesses and jurymen.

Briefs for the prosecution of the prisoners for trial were handed out to the senior barristers in rotation, and were known as 'Soup', but they rarely came the way of the newly fledged. We attended Circuit rather to watch and to learn our business, and to hope that some senior would be called back to London and bequeath his brief to ourselves. I think that during three years of going on Circuit I received two main impressions. One is that British Criminal procedure is less than fair to the Queen. Each case is presented to the jury on the assumption that a man of previously unblemished character is standing in the dock. In making private judgments of an offence by one of our friends, our children, or our dogs, we are quite properly and logically influenced by the fact that it is one more in a series of such offences. 'He has gone and done it again', we say, even before the evidence connecting culprit and crime is laid before us, and nine times out of ten we are right. But the Queen, even when she knows, through her police, that one of her subjects has already stolen money from an offertory-box fifteen times, is not allowed to say : 'He has gone and done it again'. And the jury, with a supposedly blameless person before them, and reluctant to believe in so mean a crime as robbing offertory boxes, are inclined to take the prisoner's word for it that he was in the church late at night for the purpose of admiring the Norman arches by moonlight. Had the Queen been allowed to tell them of the fifteen previous robbings of offertory boxes, they would have exclaimed in unison : 'Norman arches my foot !' I am not criticising the procedure ; it matters more that the tenth man who for once was abstaining from offertory boxes should not be con-

victed than that one of the other nine should from time
to time be wrongfully acquitted. But the fact remains
that the Queen is handicapped in her task, and the
prisoner favoured. Incidentally, I was always full of
admiration at the way a police-inspector, with a list of
the previous fifteen convictions in his pocket, would
preserve his poker-face when giving evidence against
the man in the dock.

The second of my two main impressions was that
ninety per cent of the prisoners sent for trial to County
Assizes are mentally below par. Occasionally a shrewd-
looking embezzler would scan the jury with clever,
calculating eyes ; but for the most part the offenders,
whether arraigned for crimes of dishonesty or lust, wore
dull, feeble looks, open mouths, dropped jaws, hanging
under-lips, puzzled or apathetic eyes — these were all
the average prisoner had to oppose to the firm, clear-cut
countenance of Mr. Arthur Denman, the Clerk of the
Assize, facing him from a chair immediately beneath
the Judge himself. Denman had a skin of vellum, and
a patrician, hawk-like face ; he turned his head like a
bird, too, instantly to quell this or that movement or
murmur such as continuously disturb a crowded court of
Law. Should the prisoner raise his head subsequently
to look over and beyond Mr. Denman, he was eye to
eye with the Judge — 'Long' Lawrence, perhaps, long
in face and long in body, with Goering's upper lip and
a countenance half-shadowed, like King Charles the
Second's in his portraits, by the overhanging thickness
of his wig. There was little enough in the Judge's
aspect to hold a prisoner's gaze ; the jury were more
promising objects for scrutiny, some of them with
features almost as indeterminate as his own ; but I

often got the feeling that, to the prisoner, Mr. Denman represented the veritable face, blanched, thin-lipped and impassive, of that Justice which leant so far towards the culprit's side.

There was indeed one occasion when a typical 'old lag' appeared in Court, Bill Sikes himself, broken-nosed, thick-eared, with a powerful jaw and little dart-ing eyes. But it was in the jury-box ; and he wore a neat dark suit and a clean collar, and looked as smug as a choir-boy as he trooped into the box with the rest. The case was hardly opened when a police-inspector whispered to Mr. Denman, and Mr. Denman, after a bird-like turn of hi⸱ head towards the jury-box, whispered to the Judge ; and the Judge informed Counsel that a fresh jury must be sworn. So the jury trooped out again and retired, and in a few minutes were recalled and resworn, but without Bill Sikes. By some error the name of the old convict, who had spent half his life in prison, had been retained in the list of citizens liable to be summoned for jury duty. Had the police not recognised him, would he have been for convictions or acquittals ? It is likely that at any rate he would have seen through the piteously improbable tales told by the habitual offenders. Denman, though somewhat rigid and aloof, could be helpful and con-siderate to young barristers, but on one occasion he gave me the worst five minutes of my short career at the Bar. A Norfolk solicitor had sent me, for my father's sake, the brief to prosecute a man for setting fire to corn-stacks. I travelled down to Norwich to find myself alone at the Maid's Head, for the Calendar was short. It was my first criminal brief, and I cele-brated it by drinking a bottle of Veuve Clicquot to my own cheek.   As I went into Court next morning, Denman leant over and, rather to my surprise, asked if I knew about the arson case.   My brief was quite clear as to the story, so I said 'Yes, thank you' and went to my seat.   My case was called first.   A wretched, hairy sort of half-wit stood in the box.   I rose to my feet, with clammy hands and brow, and in my nervousness failed to notice that the Clerk had not asked him what he pleaded.   I began to open the facts.   The Judge at once intervened.

'There is the preliminary matter to be tried,' he said.   I was at a complete loss.   The solicitor who had instructed me from a small country-town was not present, and there were no senior barristers at my side. I leant towards Denman and asked him what I was to do.   He replied, to my horror : 'You have got yourself into this hole, and you must get yourself out of it.' His thin mouth closed with a snap ; he folded his arms, leant back, and gazed into space.   There I stood, my first brief in my hand, stared at by the jury and the whole Court, without a clue as to my next move, and rejected by the one official who could have held out a helping hand.   Luckily the Judge was a kindly man — I rather think it was 'Tommy' Bucknall.   He must have heard Denman's refusal to come to my aid.

'This prisoner is said to be insane,' he said to me, 'and you must tell the jury that they are to find whether or not he is fit to plead.   Then call the Prison Doctor.' I repeated the Judge's words to the jury and called the Prison Doctor, who gave evidence that the fire-raiser was mad as a hatter.   The jury found him unfit to plead, and the case was over.

At the luncheon interval I went back to the Maid's

M

Head, determined, junior as I was, to write a letter to the Clerk of Assize, telling him what I thought of him. There I was handed a note from Denman, written the night before, but sent by error to another hotel. In it he told me that my man was insane, and offered to explain to me next morning what the procedure would be. This accounted for his behaviour in Court, but to this day I cannot feel that it excused it.

Denman himself must have had twinges of conscience, for at the next Maidstone Assizes, after I had unsuccessfully defended a prisoner on a charge of attempted rape, he sent me a note by the Court Usher congratulating me upon my handling of the case. I was pleased, for he was sparing of praise, but far more astonished, since I had no inkling of what I had done to deserve commendation. Later, he explained. Most young barristers, he said, would have cross-examined the woman who had been assaulted with a view to getting her to admit that she had provoked, or at any rate, misled her assailant, 'whereas you', he added, 'very properly accepted her story and refused to cross-examine.' Now the complainant was a plain, middle-aged woman of signal respectability who had been thrown down by a half-drunken tramp while wheeling her child in a perambulator, and no young barrister, however crude, could conceivably have imputed to her the giving of a glad eye to the rag-bag of a man who set upon her. Denman must have known this for he had seen them both ; but he wanted to say 'Sorry', and had devised this rather preposterous way of doing so. But it was kindly meant.

The biggest money I ever earned — 120 guineas out of a total of £186 during three years' practice — was in the Magistrates' Court at Dover. George Joseph was a busy Junior Counsel who shared the Chambers in which I was a pupil. When he was briefed to defend a man prosecuted for the rare offence of criminal libel, he asked me to help him, and eventually insisted with the instructing solicitor that I should be given a junior brief in the case itself. This entitled me to a fixed percentage of his own fee. Our client was a mild, inoffensive looking little man who had taken a few shares in one or more of the original companies formed to develop the Kent coalfields. He was no fool at business, and had detected a fishy flavour in certain transactions by a Mr. A., the promoter and Life Governor of that group of companies. So he circularised his fellow-shareholders and suggested an enquiry. Mr. A. retorted by laying an information against him for criminal libel. Criminal libel differs from civil libel in that the truth of the facts asserted does not constitute a defence. The 'crime' lies in writing and publishing words likely to cause a breach of the peace. Now if you publish to the world that I am a thief, I am no less likely to be provoked into hitting you over the head if I am in fact a thief than I am as a person of probity. In fact, more likely, since an innocent man can afford to laugh it off. For this reason the defence is tricky, for who can say what is, and what is not, calculated to cause a breach of the peace in any given case? George Joseph decided that he must give the prosecutor such a grilling before the magistrates that he would be unwilling to enter the witness-box a second time at the Assizes. With this end in view we spent many laborious days studying the constitution and financial transactions of the whole group of

Mr. A.'s companies. We found our hard work highly rewarding. In the little Magistrates' Court at Dover I sat beside Joseph for several days, handing him ammunition for his cross-examination of Mr. A. Three magistrates sat on the dais like stuffed dummies, red-faced from the implacable winds of South-East Kent, and stolidly expressionless, for, as was evident, they never understood a word of what it was all about. Mr. A. had manipulated his inter-company affairs with skill, but Joseph drove him or drew him at will, urbane, smiling, but relentless, until all his tangled schemes lay bare. Mr. A. was a big man with a big head, gold-rimmed spectacles and a formidable jaw. He entered the box imperially, an offended monarch ; but he left it in disorder. It was my first experience of watching the slow discomfiture of a confident bully, and I must have been fascinated, for at one point Mr. A. suddenly appealed to the Bench.

'I object to being stared at by Counsel,' he said.

'If a cat may look at a King, mayn't a barrister look at Old King Coal ?' I asked him. Joseph frowned at me, and nobody was amused but myself and the Gallery.

The magistrates, obviously at sea over the whole matter, committed our client for trial at the Assizes. A K.C. was briefed to lead Joseph, which swelled our fees ; but Joseph had guessed truly. Mr. A. could not face a second cross-examination ; the prosecution offered no evidence at Maidstone, and our little client was discharged. What he had written, stood.

Joseph's room at 4 Harcourt Buildings looked out upon the pleasant lawns of the Inner Temple, as did the larger book-lined room of Sir Gerald Hohler, K.C.

But the third room, in which I sat at a table facing
C. M. Pitman, looked into the narrow canyon of Middle
Temple Lane, and was a drab little box in which to
spend the day, could any place have seemed drab
inhabited by 'Cherry'. 'Cherry' had been a celebrated
stroke of Eton and Oxford and Leander crews, and I
had paid him £100 for the privilege of being his pupil
and occupying a chair in his Chambers. He had still to
make his own way at the Bar ; the briefs that came
his way were neither numerous nor important ; I
could undoubtedly have seen more work in many
another set of Chambers ; but nowhere in all the Inns
of Court could I have been so happy. As a mentor,
'Cherry' had a knack of putting legal complexities into
intelligible nutshells, with fresh and humorous illus-
trations of his own invention ; even the far more
learned Joseph would bring moot points for 'Cherry'
to settle with an impromptu blow upon the very head
of the nail. His approach to the law was always that
of an advocate with a client, never that of a jurist with
a principle. He could present the pith of a case to a
jury in a few words as short of syllables as was practicable, and with his pleasant vibrant voice and endearing
good looks he seemed cut out for distinction at the
Common Law Bar. But he had no ambition and a
streak of contentment next-of-kin to indolence, and
came to rest in the honourable but not exalted post of
Official Referee. As a man to sit opposite to, however,
'Cherry' was unique. His wit, of the merry not dry
description, never failed. He had a rare and genuine
interest in other people's concerns. Cheerfulness never
had to break in, for it was always there, be the briefs
never so few. We were not seldom unemployed in

our den, but we always had fun. When other topics
failed, we strafed Joseph. It was a godsend to two Old
Blues, still bluer from their cold baths and scorn of
greatcoats, to have as stable-companion a bottle-
shouldered, flat-footed Jew, who had been to neither
public school nor University, who had never played a
game or walked a mile in his life, and who packed a
hot-water bottle when he visited Brighton for the
week-end. We let him off nothing, and he in his turn,
clever, quizzical and amused, enjoyed trailing his coat
for us. Secure in his pride of race, he could afford to be
our butt. On one point he admitted our superiority.
A tailor used to visit our Chambers to try on Joseph's
new clothes, and I was invariably summoned to be
present as arbiter between the tailor and himself. I
can still see the tailor's gestures of despair behind
Joseph's back, as he described curves in the air to show
me the hopelessness of getting a coat to hang properly
from the hock-bottle that took the place, in Joseph's
anatomy, of shoulders.

It would be ungrateful to recall these Chambers in
Harcourt Buildings without a tribute to the Clerks.
Barristers' Clerks are famous for resource and fidelity
alike, and Hughes, his son Charlie and George were
among the best. Hughes, with a big head thatched with
thick grey hair, looked like a benevolent university
professor ; Charlie looked like his father, and George
like a clean-cut, rising young Tory. All had finished
manners ; and from my first day Hughes took me under
his wing with a perfected blend of fatherliness and
deference. Clerks must know every detail of Court
procedure ; but their most delicate task is to fix their
employer's fees, and to convey to instructing solicitors,

without actual falsehood, that Counsel are a great deal more in demand than is in fact the case. Briefs, old and new, have to be arranged with artistry on mantel-shelf and side-table so as to make the best showing when a solicitor is due for a consultation ; and the blank pages of an engagement book must be flipped through with an anxious frown, as if already overloaded with appointments. If it was sometimes nerve-racking to sit, during an idle spell, listening to Hughes telling a client on the telephone that Mr. Pitman, who had no engagements, could not possibly see him until Friday, Hughes knew exactly how far he could go. The client always turned up, and the fee was suitable for a Counsel who had only an hour on Friday to spare. The genuine friendship of these three men added much to the amenity of life in Chambers, and when I announced my engagement to Hughes, he said : 'I guessed as much, from your voice when you spoke to the young lady on the telephone.' As the young lady had not rung up our Chambers more than a couple of times, and my guarded replies in the Clerks' cubby-hole cannot have been more than : 'All right, six o'clock', Hughes' perceptions must have been delicate indeed.

Another beautifully played part in the Bar comedy, which I never ceased to admire, was the rôle of instruct-ing solicitor. The examinations for a call to the Bar are child's play compared to those which must be floored by a candidate for enrolment as a solicitor. These lawyers knew their law indeed, but being liable to be mulcted in damages for negligence should they slip up in their advice to a lay client, it is their practice to cover themselves by taking 'Counsel's Opinion'. In submitting a case for the Opinion of Counsel they take good care to refer Counsel to every Statute and Case which could bear on the point at issue, so doing most of his work for him. But, knowing the correct answer, they are most careful, while making Counsel's own conclusions foregone, never to prompt him in so many words. And when Mr. Mowll of Dover, or a partner in Robb and Welch (who flourished as lawyers in despite of their discouraging names) arrived in person for a consultation, their deferential bearing and tactful concealment of their own mastery of the law were a pleasure to watch. It was the more admirable in that in fact solicitors hold the fortunes of junior barristers in their hands ; it requires delicacy and a real love of traditional decorum for the paymaster to pay so much respect to the piper he pays.

It is not surprising, having regard to the slenderness of their claims to superior learning, that barristers have hedged themselves about with almost priestly defences. Wig and gown are vestments ; the lawns and Halls of the Inns of Court have the tranquil apartness of a cathedral close ; and by the time a solicitor had passed beneath the arcades and by the little wig-shop, and skirted Pump Court, with a glance at the tail-coats and top-hats dotting the great lawn, he had become conscious of his own bowler hat and of a great gulf fixed. Temples have had precincts from time immemorial — sacred enclosures which have been crossed by the suppliant, when not actually shoes in hand, with a quickening sense of an approach to mystery ; and the Inner and Middle Temples, Lincoln's Inn and Gray's Inn, have done likewise. None but another lawyer, no less learned than the man he seeks out, is permitted to visit a barrister in one of these Courts, up one of these collegiate staircases, on the business of the law. A litigant may be summoned to a consultation in those guarded Chambers, but only in the presence of his solicitor, and his humble part is to pay two lawyers for services which in America are rendered by one. The system is historical, illogical, picturesque and expensive, played out with perfect gravity by all parties, and there can be no greater tribute to British law, and to the potency of ritual, than its acceptance by the public with cheerfulness and even pride.

There can be no easier transition for a young Oxonian from Colleges and quadrangles to life in earnest than by way of the Inns of Court. Once again he sees his name painted at the foot of a staircase ; he lunches in a Gothic Hall, at a long, polished table, among colleagues pursuing the same branch of learning ; he strolls again upon summer lawns ; he belongs to a privileged community. There was a tradition of friendliness between seniors and juniors : why should Hal Dickens, a Cantab several years my senior, have so smoothed and enlivened my early days with his advice and good fellowship ? The profession itself is highly competitive ; many are called but few are chosen ; yet nowhere can there be so little jealousy, so much readiness to give a helping hand. On one occasion, it is true, I met with disenchantment. A rising young Silk, whom I had casually met at Oxford, greeted me with unexpected warmth. 'My dear fellow, I am delighted that you have joined us ; if ever I can be of use, don't hesitate to come to my Chambers.' I was flattered, and more so when, on occasions, this man already marked out for great things deliberately chose to sit by me at luncheon in Hall, and to talk to me at

the full stretch of his gifted mind. There came a day
when he put his arms round my shoulders as he settled
at my side. 'My dear fellow, I want you to do me a
favour ; will you come and speak for me at W. ?'
where he was fighting a by-election. I told him that I
should have liked nothing better but for the insuperable
obstacle that I was on the other side in politics. He
looked at me in amazement : 'They told me you were a
keen Liberal !' The next time we met he nodded and
passed by ; in a few weeks even the nod was omitted.
I had had my first experience of humbug, and to have
met it in a man of his calibre and reputation was dis-
illusionment indeed. He for his part, although deprived
of my assistance and support, pursued his bleak, un-
swerving way to the very highest positions open to a
political lawyer. He achieved all his ambitions, save
colleagues to call him by his Christian name.

On my first day in Chambers, 'Cherry' Pitman led
me round the Law Courts to have a look at the Judges.
As we emerged from those grim Betjemanic halls and
corridors into the dusty sunshine of Fleet Street 'Cherry'
said : 'So what is the first thing to do if you want to
succeed at the Bar ?' I had no reply. 'Put your face',
said 'Cherry', 'under one of these new motor-buses.'
Our last call had been upon the Court where Lord
Cozens-Hardy, the Master of the Rolls, presided, and I
saw what 'Cherry' meant. But I had been less consoled
by the Judges' lack of good looks than dismayed by
two beards and one lank walrus moustache. Ridley J.
and Bailhache J. both wore beards, but a judicial air is
given to a man by the set of his mouth and upper lip,
and when these are invisible, not even the wig can save
a face from insignificance.

Consider the long line of seventeenth-century portraits of lawyers and divines, the Cokes and the Lauds,
how feeble and characterless they appear with their
small trim beards, and no upper lips or mouths or chins
to record and communicate the lines that belong to ripe
and proven men, masters of their chosen calling.   But
the moustache was more disastrous still.   Fletcher-
Moulton L.J. had a prodigious reputation, not only
for learning in the law, but for his grasp of those
daunting problems of physics or mechanics which
bedevil patent cases and the like.   It was all the more
grievous that this able Judge exhibited a drooping,
ragged moustache, with pendulous, protracted ends,
which gave him an air, not of an alert, judicial lawyer,
but of a sad Crimean veteran mumbling on an alms-
house bench.   No, the Judges of my time hardly looked
the part ;   even Darling J., for all his wit and swift
business-like handling of a case, had something finicky
and spinsterish about him, with his affected-seeming
play of neck and hands, and Avory J., with small sharp
features and Cockney vowels, was not, so far as sound
and sight went, altogether wig-worthy.   Only the
Lord Chief Justice, Alverstone, filled the bench to fill
the eye ;   his great, rounded, wrinkled brown forehead
seemed to curve away for ever when he pushed back
his wig in his impatience ;   for the Lord Chief could
be irritable and barked at Counsel, but with witnesses
he was patient and considerate, and at the Assizes
humane.

But there were good looks in the offing, to embellish
the Bench a few years later.   Eldon Bankes, K.C., not
yet a Judge, was a man of such faultless good looks,
cast in the traditionally legal mould, that one felt there

must be a catch in it : is a man given height and proportion, regular, aquiline features, a powerful head, a
serene brow, with no countervailing drawbacks to so
much perfection ?   But there was no catch in it ; Eldon
Bankes was all that he appeared to be ; and in course
of time became the handsomest Judge of the century.
Then there was Romer, K.C.   Chancery Silks are
attached to a single Court, so there was no difficulty, in
an idle half-hour, in finding this commanding figure in
action.   If Bankes was the fair beauty, Romer was the
dark one, and of the two, for all Bankes' impeccability,
I should, had I been a girl, have dreamt of Romer.   The
Chancery Courts, with their endless reading of affidavits,
and moth-eaten, bearded juniors, were not places of
entertainment ; but when Romer was up, flashing
intelligence from his dark, purposeful eyes, a young
barrister could linger there entranced.   He, too, was
to beautify the Bench.   Sir Edward Carson was not,
perhaps, strictly handsome ; his chin was too long, the
bones of his strong jaw too palpable beneath the skin.
But there was grandeur in his forceful masculine looks,
and a false witness, could he think at all when face to
face with that formidable man, may well have thought
of Mephistopheles.   Carson's brogue underscored all
his questions, and his pauses were heavy with foreboding.   It was such a pause that came after his question
to a witness :

'Are ye a heavy drinker ?'

'That's my business.'

'Yerse — but have ye any other business ?'

Carson was the foremost advocate of my time ; or
was it Rufus Isaacs ?   Isaacs was mostly engaged in
commercial cases ; a courteous, genial man, with the

aquiline good looks of his ancient race. He, too, could dominate a Court of Law, and when the Marconi scandal broke there was not a member of the Bar, whatever his politics, who did not swear to Isaacs' honour, be his judgment what it might. Practice at the Bar, with so many opportunities for trickiness, exposes an advocate, year in and year out, to keen-eyed, keen-witted rivals, but the integrity of this brilliant man was never in question. If he was for once an ass, he was never a knave.

Then there was F. E. Smith. Legend already surrounded this slim, dapper figure, hardly recognisable at first glance in wig and gown, since the sleek ebony hair was concealed by the wig, worn a little jauntily. His sombre eyes and clean-cut features were lawyer-like enough ; only the mouth lacked the set precision of a typical legal face. The lips were slightly ajar, as if about to close upon a cigar ; at moments shaped to insolence or disdain ; sometimes weary. I had the luck to hear 'F. E.' and Horatio Bottomley, for once not in the dock, successively address a jury. 'F. E.' was trenchant, rapid and authoritative, but the rascally Bottomley, with sagging jowl and capacious skull, was silkily persuasive, speaking low, in a surprisingly culti-vated voice — an elderly injured gentleman asking for no more than bare justice. I forget the issue of the case, but Bottomley's performance was the most telling address to a jury I have listened to.

It is curious, on looking back fifty years, to remember with what little consideration of alternative careers I slipped into the Law. The City or industry were never so much as discussed : we had few, if any, acquaintances engaged in any kind of business. Diplomacy had been thought of, but the examination was exceedingly stiff, and I lacked means ; the Civil Service, which might have suited my disciplined, subordinate temperament, gave no chance of restoring the family fortunes. For Cranmer Hall and the Cranmer estate were always in the background of my father's thoughts and mine, and while I never saw myself as a whole-time squire or farmer, my childish memories were vivid, and I liked to think that some day I should be scheming how to make the pheasants fly higher from our own familiar woods. All my active pleasures had their source in the countryside, and my visual enjoyments too ; I never thought of our Norfolk park and manor as pasture or plough, but as landscape for the eye, changing colour with the seasons and the sun, and founded on the light dry soil which partridges love. I foresaw good sport there, if I could make money ; and I remembered, as well, the yew hedges, and the many-walled garden, and the great chestnut trees in blossom. Cranmer had a strong, if intermittent, pull upon me, and being, as I say, ignorant of most of the ways in which money is made, I turned to the Bar as to the one profession which could, in those days, bring moderate fortune. I had no vision of Judgeships, still less of Lord Chancellorships, for party politics had no charms for me. I was at the Bar to make money, and to make money I forsook it.

I have said that the pull of Cranmer was intermittent, for I left Oxford with far other thoughts than of that forsaken home. I was elated and shaken and sundered from reality by a love-affair, of the high poetical kind, with no warm touch of earth, no place in it for kisses or caresses, an airy-fairy flying folly, but obsessive, devastating and exhausting. Romance had me in thrall,

as implacably as any Belle Dame sans merci, and I
soared even while I suffered. The thing happens, I
suppose, to many young men, but not all of them, it is
to be hoped, have to sleep in their father's dressing-room
when the spell is upon them. It sounds a mild enough
purgatory, but a room of my own, even a locked
drawer for my letters, could have spared me much
nervous strain during that dreary winter when, sluggish
from overwork and desperately love-lorn, I lived with
my family in an overcrowded flat on the Embankment.
My unoccupied father's simplicity, affection and unbounded curiosity was the last thing I wanted in my
complicated predicament, and not all my mother's tact
and understanding could mitigate the embarrassments
of that shared shaving-glass. My father never could
grasp that his children's letters should be left on the
slab in the hall, and not picked over and handed by
himself with an air of enquiring sympathy to the re-
cipient. It was indeed the winter of my discontent.

In the end my mother's wisdom prevailed over the
demands of economy, and by the time I was called to
the Bar I was living happily in a bachelor colony in
Bedford Court Mansions. Francis ('Timmy') Jekyll
rented a high and spacious flat in those red-and-yellow
Bloomsbury buildings, and sub-let bedrooms to three
or four of his friends. Timmy himself had a not very
exacting job in the British Museum close at hand ; he
was eager and humorous, the best of companions in the
cheap seats at the opera or over a mug of beer at the
Old Gambrinus. Here we would sit beneath the antlers,
clasping our grey, lidded, earthenware mugs and strain-
ing our ears to catch what Belloc was saying to
Chesterton at the corner table. We never did hear,

since both spoke at once and laughed and rumbled continuously ; but we did not feel the smaller for the propinquity of those two enlargements of the human kind. We felt, on the contrary, a little more knowing, a shade less immature, to be sharing a waiter with such giants.

But if Timmy was a good companion, he was not an ideal landlord. For although never hard up, and keeping, in fact, a preternaturally large balance on current account, Timmy had a rooted objection to paying bills, including his own quarterly rent. It was the physical act of writing a cheque to which he could not bring himself ; life, he maintained, afforded no time for such banausic interruptions while so many pages of Bach remained to be played, at sight, on the piano in our common sitting-room. For when Timmy was not in the British Museum, he was play-ing Bach endlessly, endlessly, with true musicianly feeling but occasional stumbles and wrong notes.

The result of Timmy's obstinate refusal to write cheques was that from time to time Bailiffs appeared in our flat — small polite men who for some reason kept their bowler hats on their heads while they sat on a red-plush Victorian settee in the entrance hall. Timmy, unperturbed, would explain to the polite little men that payment was now quite out of the question, since to write a cheque with bowler hats in the hall would be to write it under duress, which no gentleman of spirit could endure. They were apologetic but remained on the settee. Whereupon Tommy Lascelles and Charles Lister and 'Bunt' Goschen and myself had to buy luggage-labels, to inscribe with our names and to tie round the clock, a chair, or a bookcase, for we had all contributed some article of use or ornament to the common pool. And so Timmy would yield, not to the threat of distraint, which only hardened him, but out of consideration for ourselves, his friends. For he had a soft heart, and the spectacle of his companions compelled to write out several luggage-labels because of his own refusal to write one cheque melted it at long last.

Timmy was 'done for' by a married couple who lived in attic rooms above our heads. On one occasion we came in late at night to find the hall strewn with garments, male and female, as well as with brushes and pots and pans. A pale and shaken husband came out of the shadows to explain that he had had 'words' with his wife, who had taken a drop too much. He had retreated to our floor, and his wife had thrown everything movable down the stairs after him. The scene and the man's story had all the squalor of an alcoholic seaside postcard ; I think we all felt a little soiled as we picked our ways to our rooms through the debris of the battlefield. The 'sanctity of the home' appeared to be less axiomatic upstairs than in Deaneries.

But we were in smooth waters when the faithful Maxlow came to serve us. He was far from a paragon and there were many grumbles, but he liked us, which is the one thing needful in a domestic, and the collar-box of the finest durable leather which Maxlow gave to me as a wedding-present must have cost more than any tips he got from me. I hope he noticed how well it looked at the vulgar and shameless, but then customary, display of wedding-gifts in Dorchester House.

The population of Bedford Court Mansions was fluid, not static, and apart from Timmy, I find my

N

recollections of those pleasant years most pervaded,
perhaps, by the figures of Tommy Lascelles and Bunt
Goschen. Both were working for the Foreign Office
examination — was it at Scoones' ? — and so was
Charles Lister ; but Charles was more of a bird of
passage, or perhaps his multifarious pursuits, political
and philanthropical, left him fewer evenings to share
our three-course dinners, at not more than half a crown
a head, at the Vienna Café or the 'Petit Riche'. Nowadays I wonder how it was that we did not see at a glance
that Tommy Lascelles was to be Private Secretary to
two Monarchs, for the qualities which made that
destiny inevitable were already not merely latent, but
perceptible, in him. It must be remembered, in excuse
of our blindness, that the hole for which Tommy was
the prefabricated peg is unique and not one of a class ;
that he himself hoped to be an Ambassador ; that he
carried a flavour of fox-hunting about him that did not,
in the reign of Kings Edward VII or George V, remind
us of monarchs, and that he was temporarily Wagner-
struck. Few things recall to me more vividly our
common sitting-room, lighted sunlessly by a northern
sky, to which only our warm youth could have been
so indifferent, than talk of *leit-motifs* and of those
throttling bores who vapour so everlastingly in the *Ring*.
For me Wagner is the outstanding example of an artist
who was great in spite of himself, who did not know
what he was doing : the serene loveliness or prodigious
swell of exhilaration in his operatic music, the continuous excitement of the orchestral commentary (even
when Tristan is so exasperatingly slow to die), possess a
life of their own, independent of the words or thoughts
of the actors in the drama. Indeed, an understanding of

the words sung may be a positive bar to enjoyment : who could surrender themselves to the unearthly beauty of the Flagstad's singing, in the Second Act of *Tristan*, if they were thinking of the poor, tawdry words set to that divine music ? But Tristan and Isolde at any rate are lovers, and lovers have never found words to match the level of their delectable madness : the *Ring* is another matter. For Wagner himself the music of the *Ring* was as directly inspired by his own portentous version of the *Nibelungen* legend as a clergyman who applied to me for the living of Sculthorpe was said, in a letter of recommendation, to be directly inspired by the Holy Ghost. In both cases there seems to have been some mistake. I can well believe that the Holy Spirit inspired many passages of Wagner's music, but never that such beauty was born of the long-winded Teutonic dullness in which that composer has wrapped his gods and heroes.

But these are maturer reflections ; we were young when Tommy Lascelles, who had just been, or was hoping to go, to Bayreuth, carried Shaw's *Perfect Wagnerite* in his pocket, and Bunt Goschen, who as the son of Sir Edward Goschen had music in him as a birthright, played the *leit-motifs* to him on Timmy's piano. We all took Wagner's creatures very seriously indeed, and felt ourselves to be in touch, potentially at least, with some tremendous motions of the world-soul, and what are known as 'higher things'. So that it is really no wonder that in spite of Tommy's address, and tact, and discretion, and humour, and sense of form and fitness, and skill with his pen, and just appraisement of persons, we did not foresee him at Buckingham Palace. For Wagner, in those days, can have been rarely listened to, or even talked about, in those august quarters.

Bunt (Gerard) Goschen was a treasure we all cherished. Nature had made it up to him for a certain lack of grip, a vagueness in his approach to the practical things of life, by endowing him with so warm and sunny a temperament that we basked — there is no other word — in his company. His humour was pervasive ; his jokes endearing ; his falls into love as poignant as they were recurrent. 'I think I must be numbed,' he remarked, as he played Strauss waltzes with spirit on the morning after a rejection by some beloved one. The unselfconscious friendliness of his wide-open heart, and the quickness of his perceptions where beauty or humour, not business, were in question, made Bunt the most satisfying of companions. He was ostensibly working for the Foreign Office examination, but we all knew him to be unequal to that formidable test ; and it was a kindly stroke of fate that sent Bunt, a week before the examination was to take place, skyward in a balloon. For Victor Barrington-Kennett ('B-K'), who persuaded Bunt to this adventure, was still a beginner in aeronautics ; and, descending too quickly, the balloon bumped and dragged along the ground, and Bunt was thrown out and suffered a most timely concussion.

I think it must have been Bunt's sunshine, reinforced by both Tommy's and Charles Lister's social ubiquity, that brought girls on occasion to Bedford Court Mansions, and caused our small colony to enjoy a diminutive renown among those with whom we dined and danced. There was an occasional supper-party after a theatre ; the girls were chaperoned as a matter of course ; even Viola Tree, who had already played Trilby, might not visit Alan Parsons, to whom she was engaged, with none present but ourselves, her friends and his, to safeguard her virtue. What nonsense it all was, and how much we should have enjoyed the modern freedom permitted to young men and women!

But these occasions were rare ; for simple as was the fare offered, we were one and all, except Timmy, hard put to it to live on our allowances. We could dine for half a crown, or at a pinch for a florin, in Soho, and dine pretty well ; even at the Union Club, to which I then belonged, I rarely paid more than three or four shillings for a dinner, and a good deal less for luncheon. But in the summer we all danced several times a week, and our laundry bills for boiled shirts and white waistcoats mounted up. One could shear off the frayed edges of shirt-front or cuffs with scissors once or twice, but not more ; and inking one's tendon Achilles to disguise the hole in the back of a black silk sock was a successful device only when the hole was still a small one. And it was exasperating to discover how high were the laundry standards of the footmen at houses where I stayed for the week-end. I counted on wearing the same evening shirt for two and even three evenings if there was to be no dancing, and the socks as well, but the footman when bringing early tea would take up an immaculate starched shirt, roll it up, and stuff it into the cylindrical, wicker-work laundry basket in the corner of my bedroom, with the socks thrown in. I have more than once had to retrieve the shirt, carefully unroll and flatten it, and return it to a drawer whence the footman would take it for the second time with (as I believed) a sneer.

In the Edwardian days a young man, if he were fairly presentable, could dance through a London season without being personally known to the givers of Balls. For a hostess, however grand or exclusive, needed as many men as girls at her ball, and accordingly depended upon a list of passable young men which was handed from hostess to hostess. It was enough to be on the list of one such hostess in the 'grande dame' class to receive cards for every Ball of note. I fared well enough my first season to do a good deal of yawning next day across the table at Cherry Pitman, but felt a little flat on occasions when my friends went off to some brilliant affair to which I had not been invited. If I was on Lady A.'s list, I thought, why should Lady B. have struck me off? At the end of the summer I received a large envelope from Mr. Lawrence Jones, a well-known solicitor, whose name was in the telephone book, as mine was not. It contained cards for all those Balls where my favourite partners had been waltzing while I was eating my solitary two-shilling dinner in Soho. In my note of acknowledgment I could but echo Dr. Johnson to Lord Chesterfield: 'Had it been earlier, it had been kind'.

There was one house, however, to which in those days young men were not to be admitted by the bare fact of being on a list, however respectable. The Duchess of Northumberland did not give balls, but small dances. These were much enjoyed, for the guests were few, the dancing-floor was uncrowded and the supper delicious. But the Duchess, as is understandable, had no personal acquaintance with enough young dancing men to supply even her own limited requirements. So a few ladies, preferably among her own

relations, on whom she could rely, were asked to
'nominate' young men for her dances. A preliminary
letter would arrive from a nominatrix : '*If* you were
to be invited by the Duchess of Northumberland for
the 7th, would you be able to accept?' If you said
yes, in due course the card arrived : on the night of
the dance the Duchess stood, very stately, at the head
of her staircase. Our names were called out by the
powdered, silk-stockinged servant. The Duchess did
not hold a list in her hand ; she relied on her memory
for the names of 'nominees', but it sometimes failed her.
On one occasion I was mounting the stairs side-by-side
with Daniel Macmillan. His name was announced.
The Duchess did not recognise it. Her hand was not
proffered. 'Pray, who nominated you?' she asked.
His answer was satisfactory. Her hand came out and
was shaken. It was a rather awful public negotiation, I
felt, between a hostess and her invited guest. But there
was reassurance in the figure of the kindly Duke,
beaming from a doorway, with the blue riband of the
Garter across his shirt-front. His must have been the
last pair of Dundreary whiskers to be seen in a London
ballroom ; they were reddish in colour and fascinated
us all and undeniably lent an air to the occasion. And
there was certainly no hint in his distinguished countenance of that secret sorrow which, he once confided to
my father-in-law, had shadowed his existence : for his
one ambition in life, he had confessed, was to hunt
hounds. Fate had given him the fairest opportunity, as
hereditary Master of the Percy Hunt. But unfortunately two things inescapably foiled him ; he never
could manage to blow a horn, and he never could tell
one hound from another.

Those were the days of Strauss waltzes and Cassano's band. The girls sat by their mothers, or clustered together at one end of the ballroom. They used no lipstick and little powder, and had to be loved for themselves and not for their looks when the dawn broke upon their pallid fatigue. Conversation was circumscribed ; there were topics of interest and importance to all young people which could by no means be touched upon. A rare bird indeed was a girl who was pursuing some study with serious purpose ; Ruth Balfour, cultivating bacteria in a laboratory, was a portent. Marriage was doubtless in their thoughts, as in ours, but we turned but half of ourselves towards one another ; the girls kept their mystery, and we our illusions. The mystery charmed and excited us, but taught us nothing of the art of living with a woman, or of the subtle disciplines it imposes. We got from our commerce with these guarded creatures no training for companionship, as young people get from one another today. As we walked home to Bloomsbury through the deserted streets romance protected us from those other girls who accosted us from the lingering shadows, but we shrugged them off with no perplexities about their predicament, no shock at such contrasted fates. All was sweetness and light in the lives of our ball-partners, but given, not achieved. Their way of living was theirs by grace and favour, and a delectable thing they made of it ; but their children and grandchildren, no longer privileged, seem to me to be doing even better. For they draw sweetness from things that are sour in themselves, and walk in the light by choice, aware of the shadows.

Timmy Jekyll, as an Eton boy, had sometimes been

seen at six o'clock Absence with a bunch of wild flowers in his hand and, Eton being what she is, nobody had kicked him for it; so it was not surprising that in Bloomsbury he took to Morris-dancing. But I was astonished at myself for allowing that same strain of obstinacy in Timmy that exposed us to the bailiffs to drag me to a rather sordid hall and make me hop about with uncombed strangers. We held short white wands in our hands, and mimed at sticking beans while we capered. There was a girl there with infinite allure in her eyes, who bent to the music as a sapling to the breeze, but I never spoke to her although we touched hands in the dance. But she may have lulled with her grace my sense of the ridiculous; at any rate I so far forgot my Eton-and-Oxford upbringing as to learn enough of those deplorable dances to become myself a dancing-master. For a whole winter I paid half a guinea a week to a young woman to play Morris-dance music on Wednesday nights at the Balliol Boys' Club at Hammersmith, while I instructed the compliant urchins in the art of bean-sticking. They danced so well and with such apparent enthusiasm that in the end we tied ribbons round their legs and invited their parents to a gala evening. It was all, I thought, a great success. But next week I was met by a deputation of the boys. Would it hurt my feelings, they asked, if the Club gave up Morris-dancing? It turned out that they loathed in their very souls what they had performed so gaily, and had been deeply humiliated by the ribbons.

I had been conscripted for the Hammersmith Boys' Club by Edmund ('Bear') Warre and Maurice ('Bongie') Bonham-Carter, and went there once a week not, I now feel sure, to do good to the boys but to do good to myself. The impulse towards self-discipline is stronger in many of us than the impulse to serve others ; I was using these cheerful boys as a means of self-improvement. I never failed to enjoy myself in their company, and yet I never got over the feeling that Wednesday was a 'black' day in my week. I had to start for Hammersmith as soon as I got home from work and I had no dinner ; and not even the strong whisky-and-soda provided by Mr. Eden, that fine un-parsonic parson, in his rectory in Goldhawk Road, could reconcile me to these trifling discomforts. It seems absurd, on looking back ; but although we were ready to put up with any kind of hardship in the pursuit of sport, my generation was not accustomed, as all of us today, to take in our stride even minor disruptions of our comfortable habits. It was a realisation of this weakness of ours that caused four Etonians, about this very time, to make a new departure in Club-running which has had an enduring success. Alfred Wagg, Arthur Villiers, Edward Cadogan and Gerald Wellesley, who had founded the Eton Manor Club at Hackney Wick for the benefit of boys whom the Eton Mission Club, being run by the clergy, refused to admit, had the acumen to see that, if they were to attract all the helpers they needed to the East End, there must be no 'Black Wednesdays' in their friends' diaries. So they built a comfortable dwelling-house for themselves as a wing of the Club, and a philanthropist's evening at the Manor begins with a good dinner and a glass of champagne, and ends, after a couple of hours spent with the boys beyond a green baize door, with drinks and gossip round the fire. Finally there is a bed, bath and

breakfast in place of the dreary last bus or train back to
the West End. It is small wonder that the Eton Manor
Club has flourished and become renowned. Helpers
go there for the sake of the boys, not to mortify themselves, and are in no danger of the corruption that may
come from feeling meritorious. In the course of time
even the clergymen at the Mission were won over to
admiration ; or maybe they had come across the story
of the Syro-Phoenician woman.

IX

A THING that I can by no means remember at this distance of time is how I came to be convinced, during the period of which I am writing, that a war with Germany was a probability about which I, as an individual, must do something. I had joined the Eton Volunteers at the bidding of my tutor, Charles Lowry, who was the Commanding Officer, but drilled and paraded and went on field-days as a corvée, mildly mitigated by our habit of humorous self-mockery when in uniform. No thought of military training ever crossed my mind at Oxford. But whether it was talks with George Lloyd, whom I used to meet at Pixton and elsewhere, or with Aubrey Herbert, into whose soul the iron of Bismarck had entered, or reading *The Riddle of the Sands*, or reports of the gallant stump-oratory of Lord Roberts, some leaven or other began its work on me soon after I came to London, and I found myself under compulsion to join the Territorial Army, and with a curious foreboding that it would some day be for business. Luckily the Inns of Court Volunteers, the ancient 'Devil's Own', had a squadron of cavalry, and the pleasure of riding once again more than made up for the constraints of drill and parades. We did riding-school at Knightsbridge Barracks under a rough-riding Corporal of Horse, at the cost of a sixpenny tip to the trooper whose horse we borrowed, and excellent fun and exercise it was ; and we drilled as a troop on Blackheath Common, charging about at most unorthodox speeds. At Whitsun we spent three days in camp at Bisley, where the cuckoos woke us before dawn ; and in August we trained for a fortnight on Salisbury Plain, where the wild flowers reached to our horses' knees. I rode an old white horse called Jack, about whom Private Ainger had nightmares. Ainger rose in the night and trod upon our faces, tugging at the tent-pole and insisting that Jack was in the tent. I was unfairly blamed for these nightly disturbances. 'But it was Ainger, not I who had a nightmare,' I protested. 'Yes, but it was your horse that Ainger thought was in the tent.' They reasoned like women or voters. Private Bonham-Carter ('Bongie') was well liked, but reputed to have no sense of humour. It seems that when told his horse had a head like a stag, he had sharply replied, 'Not in the least, it has no horns.' The missing humour was supplied, unconsciously but visually, by Private Im Thurn, when kneeling to groom his horse's hind-heels. A tail lifted above his close-shaven head, upon which fell that which fell, as Kipling would have said.

The discipline of the Squadron, the standards of turn-out, of split-second punctuality, of saluting and 'jumping to it' were terrific. I saw nothing like it in after years when brigaded with regular cavalry regiments ; stories of the Guards at Caterham are more in line with the 'Devil's Own' tradition in my day. Only in the mess-tent at dinner did we relax and become human beings. But those long hours of grooming horses and cleaning saddlery, often rewarded on parade with heavy fatigues for one speck of dust, stood me in good stead when I later held a Commission in a Yeomanry regiment. Precise knowledge of the time and effort required by the men in the ranks for each separate task, as well as of the secret fountains of 'eye-wash', is invaluable to an officer. To exercise command justly it is very necessary to have stood in a soldier's shoes.

My troop-leader was W. Field, a small, wiry, spectacled man whose civil occupation I forget, but whose knowledge and enthusiasm in cavalry matters were outstanding. Field was a dedicated man ; he foresaw war and prepared himself for it unremittingly. When it came, he was rejected for that active service to which all his toil had been directed on account of defective eye-sight. It all but broke his heart ; but he loyally devoted himself to training others to go for duty's sake where he would have gone as a lover to his love.

The same tragic fate awaited Major Emil Haag, who lectured us on cavalry tactics in Stone Buildings. Haag, who was of German origin, a handsome, flaxen-haired, blue-eyed man with a strong, determined face, was a Major in a Hussar regiment. He also, who knew his countrymen, had no doubts about the coming war. His lectures were fascinating ; he inspired me, at any rate, with enthusiasm for the *arme blanche*. At his bidding I studied a French officer's day-to-day analysis of the conduct of a Contact Squadron ; he introduced me to Colonel Swinton's classic, *The Defence of Duffer's Drift*. He took half a dozen of us to Salisbury Plain, to spend two nights with the regular cavalry and to be examined in field tactics for Certificate B. We were

entertained in the Sergeants' Mess, as a tribute to our
gentility, and treated to mugs of beer laced with whisky.
It made us enormously merry. Next day Haag rode
out with us on to the plain. He was expected to
examine all the candidates that day, but Haag had his
own ideas of thoroughness. I was the first on the list,
and my examination continued from morning till dusk.
I had to attack positions and to defend them ; to send out
patrols ; to receive and to act upon startling messages
handed to me by Haag ; to lead the party at full gallop
from point to point, 'making use of ground and cover',
and, after every set problem, to give a short lecture
to the other candidates explaining the reasons for my
solutions. Haag's cold blue eyes remained for me
expressionless ; he made no comment or criticism,
although inviting both from my companions ; he was
quiet, courteous and inscrutable. We returned to
London that night, all but myself with the whole thing
to do again. One of my friends said : 'You did well ;
I saw his eyes gleam.' I had not seen any gleaming,
but in the event scored 95 marks out of 100 for the
day's work. When war broke out, Haag, most able,
most studious, most professional of cavalrymen, was
treated like Prince Louis of Battenberg. Because of his
German name and ancestry, he was forbidden to serve
at the Front. Some word reached me of his despair,
but none of how his signal capabilities were made use of.
Perhaps, had he served with his regiment, his despair
would have been only postponed. In the early days of
the Battle of the Somme, when the 1st Cavalry Division
bivouacked, on one hour's notice to march, among the
poplar groves of Querrieu, the officers of an Hussar
regiment were suddenly called to the Colonel's tent.

We believed that orders to ride through the Gap must
have come ; we hung about for news, our feelings
flying 'all ways to onc't'. The officers emerged from
H.Q. We eagerly questioned them. Yes, it had been
a momentous occasion. The regiment had decided in
future to accept no subaltern with less than £400 a year
of his own. Nothing short of this, it had been agreed,
could enable the —th Hussars to regain the Polo Cup.
Had Haag been present, he would surely have felt even
more desperately sick at heart than a mere Yeomanry
subaltern like myself.

The 'Devil's Own' Squadron rode with short rifles
slung round their bodies, the butts supported by leathern
buckets. But swords hung from our saddles (as
H.R.H. the Duke of Connaught had to be reminded
when he came to inspect a cavalry machine-gun unit in
the third year of the first Great War.

'Gentlemen, where are your swords ?' he asked even
before greeting the Colonel, who stood with his officers
at the gate of a meadow.

'On our saddles, sir,' replied the Colonel. The war
was won, all the same). When charging about Salisbury
Plain we drew these swords, and it was upon them,
rather than upon our rifles, that Haag and our other
instructors taught us to rely. Mounted infantry had
been all very well in the Boer War, but an Uhlan patrol
on reconnaissance must be scattered by the suddenness,
the speed, the determination of our attack with cold
steel. The eyes of the German generals, who had
nothing to see with but their cavalry, must be put out
with needles and by hand. That was only forty-five
years ago. We made jokes in those days about the
'bow-and-arrow' school of thought at the War Office.

For how many centuries had sword and lance been known ? An arrow is at least a projectile, and the bow-and-arrow generals were thinking on more modern lines than we.

My success in Major Haag's examination gave me a comfortable sense of security. If ever the time came, I hoped to be a competent, perhaps even a brilliant, charger of Uhlans. The time never did come, but I was to spend an appreciable part of my life in behaving as if it might, and in feeding, watering, grooming, inspecting, selecting, casting, making much of, coaxing, and swearing at, horses. Riding has always been a delight to me ; but the 'war-horse' is a figment of poets. If I learnt nothing else in the ranks of the 'Devil's Own', I did learn of the utter unsuitableness of horses for war. Mules, yes ; because if the rations do not arrive, mules make their own arrangements and eat old boots or what there is, but horses wilt within an hour or two. A horse's stomach is too small for his size ; he must be fed at impossibly close intervals for a genuine campaigner. (He also stamps on your feet if you lead more than three of him to water unbitted on a rope, but that is a personal grudge of my own and not part of the charge of unfitness for war.)

Most of my contemporaries did not share my military presentiments. They joined up only when war broke out, and then belonged to 'Kitchener's Army', not to the plodding Territorials whom Kitchener so deeply distrusted. Ironically, they found themselves Colonels and Majors when those of us who had trained for six years or more before 1914 were still Captains and Subalterns. For although we Yeomanry officers were received by our brothers of the Regular

o

Cavalry with great warmth and kindness, there was to
be no promotion for us if a Regular officer of equal
seniority was available, whether or not he could read a
map, write an order, or take in the lie of the land. On
the other hand, it was upon Kitchener's men that the
brunt of the fighting fell. We of the Yeomanry may
not have achieved promotion or glory, but our chances
of survival were tenfold those of the gallant laggards
who came so late and died so soon.

But I must return to the period I am recalling. I had
then, fortunately, no inkling that all my enthusiasm for
the 'Devil's Own' must come to nothing. And even
that enthusiasm was not invulnerable. On the last day
of his last Whitsun Camp at Bisley (for I was to take
a commission in the Yeomanry) L/corporal Jones, his
heart and mind being elsewhere, made an impatient and
insubordinate reply to his troop-leader, Lieutenant
Field. As a result he found himself, when the rest
of the Squadron had been dismissed, unloading the
Squadron's heavier camp equipment from wagons for
a couple of hours of the hottest afternoon of the year.
It was not a happy farewell. I returned to Bedford
Court Mansions in the worst of humours, knowing
that I had been in the wrong, but no longer caring a
damn about duty or discipline, and with a neck chafed
past bearing by those outrageous upstanding hairy
collars which half-choked the 'other ranks' in all arms
in those days. I was slowly recovering my temper, but
not my interest in military matters, in a hot bath when
the telephone rang. Could I dine at Roehampton ? I
could and I did ; and I returned to Bloomsbury at
I A.M. next morning, in a reckless taxi-cab, engaged to
be married.

The prickly collars of our uniform tunics were not the only things that disciplined our bodies in those far-off days. As a barrister, I wore full morning-dress with a top-hat every working day, and a starched shirt-front beneath it. That did not come so hard to an old Etonian, who had for years been weighted with those heavy, useless tails, but it had not yet become the thing, except for 'touts', to wear 'Roddy Owen' collars with a tail-coat, however hot the weather. 'Stick-ups', once so coveted and so proudly endured at school, lost their glamour to a barrister sweltering over law-reports in a heat-wave, but wear them he must, and in case the heat should melt them, keep a spare collar in a drawer. When not working, a young gentleman was allowed to walk through parts of London in a dark suit and a bowler hat, provided gloves were worn or carried ; but never in Pall Mall, St. James' Street, Piccadilly, Bond Street or Mayfair. Here full morning-dress was expected, for might you not meet a lady of your acquaintance ? As for smoking a pipe, even when bowler-hatted in Holborn or Baker Street, that was not to be thought of. After all, there was always Soho for the unbuttoned ; and to Soho, both for cheapness and to cool our necks, we often went.

The standard of manners demanded from us was a high one, with a prescribed ritual for its proper performance. For every dinner eaten, a visit must be paid to your dinner-hostess. In the season, when dinner-parties before dances were frequent, several Sunday afternoons had to be given up to these visits. If you were lucky and your hostess was not at home you left two small cards, with the corners turned up to indicate

that they had been 'dropped' by yourself, and not by a
servant. If your hostess was at home, you must carry
your silk hat, stick and gloves upstairs into the drawing-
room, as a sign that your visit would not be unduly
drawn out. The hat was laid upon the floor at the side
of your chair, the grey gloves slumped over its rim.
For this purpose we all possessed an elegant cane ; a
slender thing that may have worn, in its youth, a light-
blue tassel round its neck at Lord's. We probably
talked to our hostess, or to her daughters, about 'the
Follies', the most endearing, the most intimate, of all
stage people. Pélissier, Lewis Sidney, Gwennie Mars,
Morris Harvey, Marie George — has there ever been
their like, for making friends with their audiences ?
We became like children listening to a bed-time story,
watching jealously for any deviation from the accepted
text, the received grimaces, of their nightly performance.
If Lewis Sidney's eyebrow, while he was explaining
that in building a 'cello the holes in it are made first,
failed to lift at the precise accustomed second, it was
noted against him. Pélissier himself was the soul and
genius of the little troupe. His enormous fat round
face, in its calyx of Pierrot's frills, shone with grease
and gusto. 'Here comes my gentleman——' he would
interrupt himself, as Maurice Baring, tall and drooping,
made his way to his stall, for his thirty-sixth visit that
season, across our feet. Pélissier was not technically so
great a clown, perhaps, as Beatrice Lillie, or Ustinov,
or Danny Kaye — but his commerce with his audience,
his air of sharing in a joke, of being one of ourselves
but so much fatter that it was up to him to be funny,
was surely unrivalled ? And his true musicianship
added touches of poignancy, of grace, to the comedy.

As for Gwennie Mars, singing as a charlady :

> My old man was a fisherman,
> I wish he had been a militiaman,

well, it was small wonder that we talked about her, for the twentieth time, as we ate our thin bread-and-butter alongside our hat and gloves.

Or did we talk of 'the Russian dancers' (as we called them in those days) — Pavlova and Mordkin in *Carnival* ; and the shy side-glances of Nijinsky in *L'Après-midi d'un Faune* ? If so I cannot have taken much part in the chatter, for I could not view such expensive spectacles unless invited, and although both Pavlova and Nijinsky remain in my memory as Children of Light, rare and astonishing, I had then, as now, no genuine feeling for Ballet. The trouble with me has always been the traditional ballet-skirts, coupled with the dancer's distressing habit of distorting her feet in order to stand upon her toes. Civilised and even half-civilised women, throughout the centuries, have tactfully draped themselves from the waist to below the knee, since Nature has capriciously refused to women what she has vouchsafed to greyhounds. In *Carnival* Pavlova wore a knee-length tunic, that fell in little Grecian ripples, full of grace ; but clad in the conventional ballet-skirt, the greater the dancer, the harder, the more sinewy, the less feminine appear her thighs. Thighs could by no means have been mentioned at that tea-table ; nor indeed could I have found any language to express my thoughts about the shapes of ballet-dancers, for it was before the days when girls, other than dancers, had legs. So I held my tongue.

I could sometimes afford a ticket for the back row

of the gallery at Covent Garden, and unless Tom
Spring-Rice or Clegg Kelly or Ferdy Speyer were
present, or Pamela Jekyll pouring out tea, I would make
my small valueless comment on Charpentier's *Louise*,
or on *Pelléas et Mélisande*, for true enjoyment must be
exclaimed about, be it never so uninformed. But I
hope I had the sense to be silent when the subject of
painting came up, for whereas music, and some kinds
of architecture, compel a gasp or an exclamation by
immediate impact, painting demands a long apprentice-
ship in appreciation. To children, as to P.R.A.s, the
nearer a painting approaches to a coloured photograph,
the better it is. Could I have stood before the Leaders,
the Leslies, the Farquharsons, the Dicksees at the Royal
Academy with the same pleasurable feelings as before
the Constables and the Rubens at the National Gallery ?
I am not at all sure that I did not ; and that is why I
hope I joined in no conversations about pictures. Or
could it be that, in most houses where I owed a Sunday
visit, those distinguished Academicians were admired
as highly as I admired them ? 'The way Leader has
caught the light on the puddles !' 'It's the sunshine on
the sheep's backs — marvellous !' I seem to hear remarks like these, coming not from myself, but from
behind the silver tea-kettle. If so, I have little doubt
but that I beamed in agreement.

There is no dead self, among my private stepping-
stones, quite so dead as the picture-gallery self of my
twenties. It is difficult to get back under the skin of a
young man who, in no Philistine company, regarded,
for example, those slick charcoal portraits by Sargent
with almost the reverence we now accord to a drawing
by John. But discrimination, unlike the Kingdom of

Heaven, can only come by observation, and that was helped, in my case, by the friendship, gained through his children, of Mr. Robert Benson. To this enthusiastic collector, master of premeditated words with which to express and to communicate his own ardour, I owe a great deal, and if later it fell to me, as his nephew-by-marriage, to dissuade him from printing 'dear, passionate Sandro !' in the official preface to a catalogue, I did it to honour restraint in the written word, not in recoil from such warmth towards great painting. Robin Benson not only had a notable collection of his own, but was brother-in-law to Sir George Holford, and although I must confess that on my earlier visits to Buckhurst and to Westonbirt, to South Street and to Dorchester House, I was in no mood to take much notice of pictures, being already hot upon the trail of felicity, yet you cannot sojourn familiarly, breakfasting and lunching and dining, among the greatest Masters, without acquiring, even half-consciously, new and more tender sensibilities. George Holford could purr over his Rembrandts and his 'Abbé Scaglia', but I do not think he would have so often lifted up his eyes to them from his games of Patience had Robin Benson not been at his elbow, for George's heart was in the Westonbirt Arboretum or in the orchid-houses. There had been no accident to a great picture that day George was found head in hands at his writing-table, groaning aloud, beyond the reach of human comfort. A bee discovered in the Propagating-house had not yet been caught, and George was waiting, but without hope, for news.

Today the great Holford and Benson Collections, each built up by the loving care of a single individual, have been broken up and scattered, and it may well be

that many of those glowing canvases have thereby
become accessible to a greater number of picture-lovers.
But it is something to have known them in the days
when they kept company together, a lordly and exclusive set, arranged to one man's taste. Westonbirt
and Dorchester House and Buckhurst were very
hospitable houses, and gay ones, and we crowded to
them for fun, not to look at pictures. But beauty
works upon us in subtle ways, and for all the laughter
and the music and the dancing, I believe the pictures
did give a lift to our enjoyment.

Did the tea-table talk turn from pictures to politics ?
I think it is likely, for those were the years when
Lloyd George was on the rampage, loudly and vulgarly
menacing the inequalities so many of us took for
granted. Doubtless the Asquiths, Greys and Haldanes
were as determined as Lloyd George to scotch privilege,
but they were temperamentally calm and mentally
balanced men, working by reasonableness where the
Welshman used passion and prejudices. So it was
Lloyd George we called names, until he won a brief
respite with his Agadir speech, foreshadowing his later
self. But although I have no doubt I joined in abusing
the Welsh Goat over the cucumber sandwiches, I
probably picked up my cane and remembered another
engagement when the talk turned against Asquith. Or
did I stay a while and stand up for the Prime Minister
for whose family I had so much affection ? I hope so
indeed : and it is not impossible, for I remember, at a
dinner-party, once calling down the length of the table
to rebuke the great Leo Maxse for stating that every
Judge on the Bench was corruptible and corrupted.
But on that occasion I was fortified with port wine,

and did not much mind the frowning displeasure with
which my interruption was received by my seniors. I
was never a party politician, but left Oxford with a
theoretical, Platonic distrust of 'democracy', and vague
hankerings after a reformed, disinterested, unself-
regarding ruling class. Chance had it that I was much
in the company of Liberals, Asquiths and Stanleys and
their friends, and it would have been natural if, through
my enjoyment of their keen, enlightened minds, and my
deep affection for them, I had been won over to
Liberalism. But mischance also had it that, through my
very presence, on fleeting occasions, in the ante-rooms
of Government, I got glimpses of things that I was not
man-of-the-world enough to accept. I ought, I see
now, as a Balliol man scorning convention, to have
been sympathetically amused when I came down to
dinner before the other guests at a week-end party,
and caught a newly appointed First Lord of the
Admiralty leaping over the drawing-room chairs
singing :

> Yip-i-addy, i-ay-i-ay,
>   Yip-i-addy-i-ay,
> I don't care what becomes of me ;
> I'm the First Lord of the Admiraltee,
> Yip-i-addy, i-ay, i-ay.

But at the time, when the German Navy was under-
going swift and sinister enlargements, I thought this a
lamentable exhibition by a statesman alone with his
thoughts.

It was a Cabinet Minister, again, who laughed at me
before witnesses for expressing disbelief in his stories
about how much he and his colleagues disliked one
another. 'Was there no such thing as loyalty in public

life ?' I asked him, and he declared me to be innocent indeed. And so unreasonably do we react to a flick at our more private sensibilities, that I must include among these mischances this same man's peremptory order to me, in the hearing of friends of us both, to marry Venetia Stanley. How, I thought, can a man so obtuse be fit to govern ?

Venetia had dark-eyed, aquiline good looks and a masculine intellect. I delighted in her and we were close friends ; but she permitted herself, in the morning of her youth, no recourse to her own femininity. She carried the Anthologies in her head, but rode like an Amazon, and walked the high garden walls of Alderley with the casual stride of a boy. She was a splendid, virginal, comradely creature, reserving herself for we knew not what use of her fine brain and hidden heart. To hear myself publicly enjoined to marry her, even though my affections were elsewhere engaged, even though Venetia would never have looked at me, was like listening to the breaking of rare porcelain. All the same, it was Venetia who introduced me to her home and family, and to consequent enjoyment and friendships for which I am ever grateful. Alderley was not just another hospitable country-house, offering all the pleasures of riding, swimming and lawn-tennis. It had its own peculiar atmosphere, since all the Stanleys were 'characters', diverse, outspoken, independent. Lord Sheffield, a bearded sage, only emerged from his library at meal-times, to take the head of the enormous table and to tease his family and guests with a severe *viva voce* examination. Denying the existence of an omniscient Deity, he was himself omniscient. A younger brother of this sceptic was a Monsignor, the Bishop of Emmaus *in partibus infidelium.* This plump, rosy, rather greedy worldling, who knew his elder brother to be damned but approved of the table he kept, was excellent company. He liked young people and demanded no respect for his sacred office. He took me through the woods to see the grave of a yet older brother, who had died a Moslem, a long, coffin-like stone embellished with arabesques. 'He lived like a dog, like a dog let him lie', were his unbrotherly words as he turned away.

Alderley was ahead of the times in the candour, the open-eyed down-to-earthness of its inmates. The table-talk there, among the brothers and sisters, was robust and disputatious. Only when a certain famous treacle-tart appeared did the whole family revert together to sudden childhood, in a flurry of spoons. Anthony Henley, the husband of Sylvia Stanley, and that rare bird, a Balliol cavalryman, made the best jokes, very properly enjoying them himself with pump-handle laughter. He was the 'Old Honks' of Balliol, the friend of Belloc, and only equalled as a boon companion, out-of-doors or in, by his younger brother Francis, 'Young Honks', now Lord Henley. At the foot of the table, speaking low among the clear, challenging voices of her children and children-in-law, sat Lady Sheffield, looking like an eighteenth-century marquise, pretty, tip-tilted, with dark eyes and brows beneath silvery hair. She could hint ; she could confide ; she could glance obliquely ; she was wholly different from her downright brood in manner, though sharing their unwinking vision. She gave me her friendship and won my heart. And, as a foil to all these bold, forthright spirits, her daughter-in-law, Margaret Stanley, went her delicate ways, softly articulating with the precision of a born actress, alert and amused, light-footed, gracious, with a touch of the Princess. She was married to Arthur, the true-hearted eldest son whose too short life was lived, without Faith, in that upright-ness too often claimed for believers alone.

If it was to Venetia that I owe the fun and friendships of Alderley, that spacious home that reflected in its large simplicity and strength the generous, no-nonsense character of its inhabitants, I owed Venetia herself to Violet Asquith. For in those days this pair of rarities, the dark and the fair, were as interlocked as night with day. Venetia is dead ; but Violet is living, and a friendship so deeply tinged, on my side, with admira-tion, imposes its reticences. All the same, no picture of my youth would be life-like without that slender, ardent figure in the foreground.

I must, I think, have been first introduced to Violet by Archie Gordon, and my early impression of her as a girl, as I expressed it in a game called 'Epigrams', still has, for me, the ring of truth : 'Waves of shadow across a wheatfield'. It brings back to me her bright, fair hair, the chiaroscuro of her moods, the undulations of her mind, and even of her neck and hands, obeying the quick impulses of feeling that had never to wait for the right, the inevitable words. Those clear tones, with a caressing, cooing note in them, now heard by millions listening to the B.B.C., held us even then ; even then Violet, the compeer of trained minds, veiled in her femininity the bright blade of her intellect. For though never girlish, she was very much a woman, and un-consciously exacted, as Venetia did not, a touch of diffidence, a shade of deference, in our masculine approaches. Violet enjoyed, as the daughter of the

Prime Minister, too wide and diversified an acquaintance to have been the centre of a clique, but, as far as I
am concerned, I do see her in retrospect as the lodestar
of a fairly constant group of friends. Whether at
Littlestone, or Archerfield, or Vinters, or Lympne, or
at No. 10 Downing Street, there recur the faces and
figures of Venetia, and Archie Gordon, and Maurice
Bonham-Carter ('Bongie'), and Olive MacLeod, and
Blanche ('Baffy') Dugdale, the niece and biographer
of Arthur Balfour. Sometimes Reginald Farrer was
there to suppress, or Arnold Ward to frighten, me ;
her brothers came and went, more welcome to Violet
than her swains ; and at Archerfield or Downing Street
Mr. Asquith himself salted the talk at table and joined,
with a mellow literacy, in our after-dinner games. For
these games were the *clou* of our gatherings. Our
host at Vinters, Sir Reginald Macleod, Chief of his
Clan and owner of a fairy flag, could hardly sit through
dinner in his anxiety to begin them. 'And now let us
be merry', he would exclaim, straddling the hearth-rug
and rolling his R's like a Frenchman. We called him
'Waxworks' because of his pink-and-white complexion
and white cotton-wool side-whiskers, and it was difficult
to believe that this jovial, hospitable man was the
hereditary, the secular enemy of countless Macdonalds.
The games themselves were fairly exacting : epigrams
were extorted ; abstruse and abstract conceits must be
guessed ; you needed to be bookish as well as wide-
awake to hold your own in them. Casual visitors,
unexercised in our peculiar sport and disinclined to
stand on mental tiptoes after a good dinner, did not
always, I fear, appreciate the fun. But Violet, nothing
if not compassionate, knew how to temper the

sharpness of our exchanges for shy or reluctant new-
comers, and drew them in or eased them out of the
arena with a sure and gentle hand.

It was through Violet, and in Downing Street, that
I first met Margot Asquith. My opening encounter
with this celebrated woman was, to me, a little surprising. I had arrived for a dinner-party, with the
nervous punctuality of a novice, on the stroke of eight,
and found myself alone with my hostess, who was
standing on the hearth-rug in a pair of black Turkish
trousers. She shook hands warmly. 'But you will be
careful, dear Mr. Jones, won't you, not to say anything
risqué before my Elizabeth. She is so innocent. I was
innocent, too ; I knew *nothing*, absolutely *nothing*, till I
married. And I had such a difficult time when she was
born — when both my children were born — *narrow*
— do you see — much too *narrow*' — and here she
swept her hands down her flanks, compressing her
slight figure still further. It was, as Gibbon said of
Pitt's, not exactly the style of conversation to which I
was accustomed, but I hope I managed to look sympathetic, and to convince her that I was not the man to
stain the mind of a child who, in any case, was too
young to appear at the party. Later I was to learn that
it was Margot's way to express aloud her casual trains
of thought, however inconsequent, regardless of the
age, sex or standing of her hearers. I was also to
become acquainted with the goodness of her heart, the
fineness of her standards in the fundamental things, and
her moral fearlessness. When in good vein, she was as
brilliant a talker as I have heard and, though never
quite adult, had insight and perception. She was
cruelly maligned during the first Great War, and it was

her tragedy that an irresponsible tongue should have on occasions betrayed to enmity a most loyal and responsible heart. To Violet and to her brothers, who reached adulthood in their teens, the spectacle of a Prime Minister's wife sobbing on a sofa because her doctor had forbidden her to attend the Trooping of the Colour must have been a strange one ; but no oath was more binding to Violet than one sworn 'on the Puffin's head', and the affection between the two families was indefeasible. (Incidentally, Anthony Asquith's name of 'Puffin' illustrates Margot's rather slap-dash approach to Nature. When watching, with Edward Grey, some rock-pipits at North Berwick, she commented upon the similarity between their quick, darting movements and those of her own small boy. 'How right Violet was to call him "Puffin" when a baby.' She had, Grey told me, always believed the pipits to have been puffins.)

X

THIRD-CLASS week-end tickets were unbelievably
cheap in those days, and although tips were a standing
source of uneasiness and even apprehension when the
butler himself folded your clothes, a young man could
pack his bag on a Saturday often enough, and travel
down, through unspoilt country, to the serene and
spacious houses of his friends. It would be ungrateful
of me not to recall so much hospitality, so many
memories of spreading lawns and cool interiors in
summer ; of winter stubbles and high pheasants, and
the warmth and welcome of bright bedroom fires.

In Norfolk Keswick must be remembered, the home
of Mr. John Henry Gurney. This sad-faced, bearded,
distinguished man was a notable ornithologist, and all
his family were concerned with everything that creeps
or flies. Abroad, their hotel bedrooms were stacked
with foot-baths and glass jars and butter-muslin ; the
window-curtains were crawling with damp new-
hatched butterflies ; lizards and green tree-frogs escaped
into every corner ; you had to tread delicately among
salamanders. At Keswick wallabies bounded about the
lawns, and laughing jackasses derided you from their
cages. But in those days I had not yet joined the ranks
of bird-lovers ; I preferred the Gurneys themselves, the
proved friends of my later childhood, high-spirited,

eager and unaffected by their indulgent father's gentle melancholy. There were games here, too, on Sunday evening, but they had to be limited to scriptural subjects, for Sunday was very much the Lord's Day at Keswick, and although the stabbing of Agag in a charade may not on the face of it appear to be particularly edifying, it was allowed to pass. The contrast between liberal Alderley or Archerfield on the one hand, and fundamentalist Keswick on the other, was extreme, if professed beliefs were in question ; but youth has a way of by-passing credal differences, and the younger generation, at any rate, of this one-time Quaker family were unconcerned with what company I had been keeping elsewhere. And for myself, it was pleasant and salutary to be reminded, among these kindly, talented naturalists and under the wide sky of my native Norfolk, that a full and sensitive life can be led by those to whom literature and intellectual curiosity are secondary preoccupations.

Of Worlingham, the home of the Alfred Mulhollands, just beyond the southern boundary of Norfolk, I have written elsewhere. On Worlingham's wide lawns the song of birds was listened to and enjoyed, but the birds remained unnamed. Nature, so intimately known and loved at Keswick, was at Worlingham a remote fairy-godmother who provided bird-song and roses indeed, but primarily game-birds to be shot, and smooth grass on which to hit balls about. Eye and wrist and hand were in constant exercise at Worlingham, with intervals at meal-times for delicious food and incongruous philosophical speculations, on a staccato, unvaried note, by our usually laconic host. At night this hitter of balls read Kipling aloud, or played

P

'Parsifal' on a pianola-organ. And Mabel Mulholland flitted about, myopic, other-worldly, humorous, enchanting and invulnerable.

Southwards again, in Essex, lay Whitelands, near Terling, the home of Mr. Edward Strutt. This big, rugged man was the leading farmer of his day, a busy, authoritative man of affairs, who kept a warm heart for family life. I owe much to his kindness and to that of his handsome, generous, child-like wife Louisa, and more to his children. Strutts — and they are a large clan — can never be dull. They look at life with clear and humorous eyes and cannot be bamboozled; you must stick to the facts with them and be ready with your reasons; but their hearts are soft and their friendship, once made, endures. I was always happy at Whitelands, where the girls tempered the matter-of-fact precision of their masculine relations with a delicate, almost fragile, femininity that presupposed, for all its allure, no faltering of the intelligence. Edward Strutt's elder brother, Lord Rayleigh, the distinguished scientist, lived next door at Terling Place, and I have vivid pictures of the two brothers, large-headed, heavy-shouldered, laughing together on a hearth-rug, shaking their knees. (To laugh with your knees is hereditary in that family; the next generation are doing it, down in Essex, to this day.) In the days I am recording I was only an occasional visitor to Terling Place; my friend there was Willie Strutt, the youngest son, who went his own way, which was music; a high-bred, aloof character, walking alone; he died tragically young. But in after years when, through the death of the elders and the marriage of the youngers, the cheerful voices of Whitelands were hushed, I managed to get handed on to Terling Place, to enjoy the friendship and to savour the company of Robin Rayleigh and his wife, of his children and step-children. That stimulating and delightful experience does not belong to the times I am remembering, but it sprang from them, and must be noted for gratitude and affection's sake.

Lady Rayleigh was a sister of Arthur Balfour, and both at Whitelands and Terling I heard High Toryism talked by the elders and their guests ; progress and innovation in farming matters did not presuppose any kindness for Lloyd George or his budgets, or any faltering over the Lords' veto. So perhaps I kept it quiet that my next week-end was to be spent at Newtimber Place with Mr. Sydney (afterwards Earl) Buxton and his calm-eyed, witty wife. I believe the sun shone all day whenever I visited Newtimber. It stands beneath the shadowy folds of the South Downs, and has the most delectable W.C. in the world, looking out upon an ancient moat and lined with irresistible books. For all the bright sunshine, we fished the moat on Sunday mornings for the rainbow trout ; these domesticated fish, knowing that they would be immediately returned to the water when caught, and all but known by name to their owner, made no difficulties about rising to an Alexandra fly. To watch Lord Buxton casting was a lesson in perfection ; and to listen to his tranquil wisdom was to forget that Lloyd George was his colleague. But I suspect that he talked of natural history and travel, not politics. It was from Newtimber that Lord Buxton set out one summer morning in full fig to attend a Cabinet meeting. He decided to walk to the station, and, having time in hand, he sat by the way at the foot of a tree, listening to the birds. But no sooner was he in his first-class compartment than trouble began. He had sat on a nest of red ants, and the ants were beginning to eat him. He pulled down the blinds, took off his pin-striped trousers and shook them out of the window. At that moment an express-train passed in the reverse direction, and the blast it caused snatched the trousers from his hands. At each stop he pulled down the blind and clung to the door handle. The Postmaster-General arrived at Waterloo wearing a silk-hat and tail-coat, but trouserless. A guard was beckoned, and a pair of oily blue overalls from the lamp-room must have shocked Lulu Harcourt and even startled the Prime Minister when their colleague entered the Cabinet Room.

Lady Buxton had no less ready a wit than her brother Vivian (Lord Bicester) ; a wit that came pat from the topic, sharply *à propos*. It would be understandable if, looking back to bygone summers, I were to recollect most clearly the casual companions of my own age who foregathered at Newtimber to laze about the moat or to walk the turf upon those bold Downs. Hosts and hostesses, however hospitable and kind, are apt to be regarded by the young as providers to be thanked, rather than as cronies to be sought out. But the years have blotted from that scene all my contemporaries, except the Buxton girls and their brother Charlie, whereas my host and hostess still stand out, even to voices and gestures, master-figures among us, but companionable without condescension.

Another house where the elders retain an ever sharper outline as their images recede in time is Cornbury Park, once the home of the great Clarendon. It stands in the ancient forest of Wychwood, still studded with

immemorial oaks, where the gnarled and twisted thorns
are draped in old-man's-beard. Hyde added a wing
in which the beauty of proportion, all but unadorned,
is memorably displayed. The owner, Mr. Vernon
Watney, was a rich man of austere manners, a scholar
and a recluse. He had a high white forehead, neat
black beard and a formal old-fashioned address. His
wife, Lady Margaret, was a Wallop, whom I had met
through her Herbert cousins, tall and red-haired, vague
and inconsequent, with unfailing humour and tolerance.
On my first visit the contrast between Lady Margaret's
expansive friendliness and Vernon Watney's grave
reserve rather disconcerted me at the tea-table ; he
seemed to me a cold, disapproving sort of man. But
at dinner, over the port, I heard for the first time his
inimitable chuckle. (I don't think he ever laughed.)
What the chuckle was about I do not remember, but
from that moment we 'clicked', and there began one
of those not too common friendships between youth
and middle-age which can have so rare a savour.
Thereafter I was invited, a singular privilege, to his
well-guarded library, where every book in the shelves
appeared, at a first glance, to be frilled like a cutlet.
The frills were the curling ends of paper-slips, for this
indefatigable student made notes of all he read, and
filed the notes for reference between the leaves of the
books themselves. There we sat, on either side of a
log-fire, while he talked and chuckled. I delighted in
his company.

At a pheasant-shoot at Cornbury our host addressed
the guns before we started out. 'There is just one
thing,' he said. 'There is a white cock-pheasant in the
woods ; my daughter Sylvie is much attached to it, so

please do not shoot it.' Before the day was over I had
shot the snow-white bird. The last stand was after
sunset ; the long pheasants came over the dark wood
black against a red sky ; I shot one and, turning, saw
fall the sacred thing, rosy in the air, white and still upon
the ground. Vernon Watney chuckled for most of the
evening, and Sylvie had long forgotten her grief before
I was allowed to forget my crime. Studious though
he was, Watney was an expert and enthusiastic deer-
stalker. His forest at Fannich, in Ross-shire, is as
romantic to the eye as a mountain-scape by John Martin.
The hills are sudden and steep, the corries deep-
shadowed, and the sanctuary full of mystery. It was
here that I had my first shot at a stag. I missed, but
kept my head. 'That,' I said to the stalker, 'is the first
stag I ever missed.' He treated me almost as an equal
on the long trudge home. It was another deep chuckle
for my host. Watney's greatest friend was Edward
Grey, and one of the regrets of my life (after All Souls)
is that in after years I had to refuse Grey's invitation to
spend a fortnight in March fishing the Cassley River with
this pair of friends. To have made a third with these
two sages and to have learnt from them, both masters,
how to fish for salmon by day, and to have listened to
their talk by night, would have been a singular privilege.
If ever boasting comes back into fashion, I shall possess,
for my contribution, the distinction of this missed
opportunity.

Vernon Watney died the happiest of all deaths, in
a matter of seconds, upon his beloved hills. On the
surface he appeared, like other wealthy men of leisure,
to spend much of his life in amusing himself, fishing,
shooting, deer-stalking or reading for pleasure. But

with his puritanism, his austere standards, his grave unsmiling approach to his many public duties, Watney had little in common with the general run of sporting, land-owning men of that period. He was prim where they were gay, censorious where they shrugged things off, reserved where they were hearty and jolly. But beneath it all, his jokes were better than theirs, his chuckle more authentic than their laughter ; and the combination of intellect with sport, gravity with fun, gave peculiar piquancy to his companionship. His wealth was inherited and he must have enjoyed it in his way, but his values were such that he could, I think, for all his conservatism, have lived on into the present equably enough. If I am wrong about this, if there are to be no more Vernon Watneys, if 'all-rounders' cannot flourish without large incomes, then something appreciable will have been added to the price of social equality.

I have already paid tribute to Pixton, but I rarely went there without a raid into the heart of Dartmoor, where the family of my closest friend, Douglas Radcliffe, spent their holidays at Bag Park near Widdecombe, the home of Uncle Tom Cobleigh and all. It was here that I had my first day with the South Devon Foxhounds, and learnt that jumping is not the essence of hunting. To gallop down the face of a hill among boulders half-hidden by bracken, with horse-swallowing bogs, green and inviting as lawns, spread to catch you in the coombs and bottoms is exciting enough. But the beauty of this Dartmoor hunting lies in the uninterrupted view of hounds that can be had where a rolling country is naked of hedge and tree. If your hireling is blown to a standstill after breasting Hay Tor, you may dismount and slacken his girths for ten minutes while the hunt, arrow-headed with the bright dots that are hounds, snakes about the contours of the opposite hill. The hunt is all yours to see, whether you gallop or stand, and to rejoin at will. But my first taste of this commendable sport was also my last from Bag Park, for Douglas was no horseman, and it was many years before I rode over that country again from my brother's home at Windwhistle. The Radcliffe family liked to tackle the high Tors on foot, and to eat their lunch on cushions of thyme, backs to the rocks, while the buzzards watched and waited, slowly spiralling in the sky. There is something fey about Dartmoor ; so much desolation and silence seems to be unrelated to this cheerful and populous England. But Douglas' father, Mr. Alexander Radcliffe, filling our glasses after dinner, soon retrieved us from such fancies. He was a sane and sound Etonian, a family lawyer who knew everybody's secrets and told none ; his son's friend, and through his son mine, concerned with all our ups and downs at School or College ; a quiet, humour-loving, companionable man, who proved in the end to be a hero. For he lost both sight and hearing, not partially but absolutely, yet contrived to live cheerfully and usefully with no means of communication save touch.

It was high summer when I stayed at Montacute, then still inhabited by the descendants of the Phelips who embellished his native country with so dominating and majestic a home. The Phelips portraits hang in unbroken succession in the long gallery, the same features in each generation authenticating the line, and my host and his sons might, but for their tweeds, have sat for this picture or for that. It is a great house, where you would expect to be greeted by a groom of the chambers at the least, but money was scarce and Mrs. Phelips, by a happy stroke, saved the face of her lordly habitation by dressing her maids in scarlet. These bright figures, crossing the lawns with the tea-trays or backed by the dark panelling within, conserved, for I suppose not thirty pounds a year a head, the graces exacted by so much stateliness in stone. Blanche Lascelles (Lady Lloyd) was a fellow-guest, and we were young enough to agree together to see the sun rise from the top of the conical hill which stands, sudden and improbable, near by. Blanche looked like a beautiful ghost, in a diaphanous silvery hood, as she descended the stairs in the dusk, and I felt it to be an adventure. But to get out of a strange, immense house before daylight is harder than we had reckoned ; every exit was barred and locked ; and we had sniffed all varieties of effluvia from pantry and scullery and larder before we broke out at length into the coolness that comes before dawn. We were drenched with dew, but we heard the first bird, and the sun did not let us down. Nowadays her companion would have kissed Blanche on that hill-top, with no further commitment. I had to be content with a reverie.

If there was no groom of the chambers at Montacute, there was a very splendid one at Hurstbourne. He wore knee-breeches and black silk stockings with silver-buckled shoes, and his raven hair fell long over his collar behind, as he bowed, flanked by powdered flunkies, to welcome young Mr. Jones, half blind with migraine in a shabby ulster, and to bid the footmen take the battered single gun-case, the worn suitcase, the

woman's shooting-stick that had been my mother's.
Lord Portsmouth, then known as 'Lym', had messed
with my father at Oscar Browning's house at Eton for
the extraordinary and revealing reason that they were
the only two boys in the house whose fathers were
Liberals. But he never addressed me otherwise than as
'Mr. Jones', and although I have drunk his champagne,
I did not share his bottle. That bottle, of a different
vintage, stood by itself on the sideboard ; the groom
of the chambers did the replenishing from behind our
host's chair. 'Porty', as he was universally known, had
a red beard which he enclosed in a sponge-bag when
motoring. He had taste and knowledge, and had been
an Under Secretary in one of Asquith's adminis-
trations. But he was singularly unrepresentative of
the humane and unassuming family of which he was
then the head. He must have come of age, heir to
the name of that same seaport where the Great Mel
flourished, about the year that *The Egoist* appeared.
Could George Meredith have heard rumours of a young
Sir Willoughby Patterne lording it in his native Hampshire ? one whose sister — but not his betrothed —
married a scholarly, athletic walker over hills called
Vernon Watney—but not Vernon Whitford? I present
this rat for some Harvard research student to hunt in
his thesis, but however the rat-hunt ends, only a Sir
Willoughby could have called out to a gamekeeper, as
the shooters arrived at a new beat, 'Keeper, which is
the best place here ?' and announced in a clear, high-
pitched voice, when the gamekeeper indicated the most
favoured spot, 'Then I will stand here ; you place the
other guns.' Unluckily for this Sir Willoughby there
came a day when one of the party was Lord St. Cyres,

who had been a Don at the House and was no respecter
of persons. For St. Cyres had a voice like a corncrake,
and his quick follow-up with 'Keeper, which is the
second best place here, for I should like to have that ?'
was enjoyed by all but his host. St. Cyres neither was,
nor wished to be, asked again. Not the story to tell,
you may think, of a man whose salt I have eaten ; but
in truth I owed my place at his table not to this strange
specimen of a Liberal but to his kind, long-suffering,
adoring wife. Besides, it is all long ago, and I have
dulled my conscience by pretending that the story is
about St. Cyres.

Railway travel cost about a penny a mile in those
days, but even so I had to think twice before accepting
an invitation to Ellesmere in Shropshire, where Mr.
Brownlow Tower lived, with his keen-witted family,
on the edge of the mere. The girls at Ellesmere were
not Harry Cust's nieces for nothing ; there was cut
and thrust at every meal, and verbal machine-gunning
at breakfast itself, against a reassuring background of
mother's knee piety and duties to one's neighbour. On
my first visit I was green enough not to know that a
young man invited to Hunt Balls was expected to pay
the guineas for his own tickets, and was humiliated at
having to borrow from Jasper More when our kind
host asked us to fork out. Luckily the absence of a
butler, appeasable by nothing less than a golden half-
sovereign, mitigated the blow.

The mere at Ellesmere is fringed with sedges that
turn to pale amber in December, framing a reflected
amethyst ; the Welsh hills are in sight of the shooters
all day ; there must have been, I think, some crispness
in the winter air as well as in the conversation to make

my memory tingle still. And what masculine ears
could have been insensitive to the sounds of 'Sylvia',
'Averil' and 'Iris' ?

Shropshire is far away enough for a briefless barrister
and Scotland is farther still, so it must, I think, have
been after my Kent Coal case that I made my first visit
to Ardgowan, the home of Sir Hugh and Lady Alice
Shaw-Stewart. I had been to Scotland as an Eton boy,
and had heard old Lady Stewart of Grantully forbid her
footman to bring me sugar for my porridge, although
she did not call the porridge 'them'. And I had shot
grouse over dogs on the slopes above Loch Ericht, with
dear Toby Albright and his silent father, and a freckled
boy we called Leatherbelly. How can I have forgotten
Leatherbelly's real name, after grilling brown trout with
him for supper by the loch-side, where we slept in
flea-bags on the floor of a tin hut ? Drumochter Lodge
is near the top of the pass at Dalwhinnie, and since my
first visit to that austere and desolate region I have never
felt myself to be truly in Scotland until out of sight of
trees. Even the birch-trees, even the lordly Scotch firs
of Glen More (except on Sundays when the high tops,
my secret homeland, must be left to the deer) do not
quite suit my humour. For whether it is that I had a
Scottish great-grandmother, or just the Celt in me, it
remains true that I have only known the sense of real
home-coming, of treading my native soil, when the
slope behind me has shut out the valley and woods and
the small green hayfields, and there is nothing before
me but moss and heather and peat-hags and the firm,
short turf, strewn with white stones, where the ptarmi-
gan run and crouch.

Ardgowan, on the west coast south of Greenock,

stands in another sort of Scotland altogether and, if without the last enchantment of loneliness, has everything else to give. Square-built, with stately classic portico, it stands among lawns and flower-gardens that might be English but for that extra vividness, those enhanced colours, with which Scottish soil, or gardeners, astonish us southerners. After a day on the rolling moors, where the grouse on one occasion packed till they almost hid the sun, like the arrows at Agincourt, it was flannels and tennis before dinner. On the private links Sir Hughie gave me my early lessons in golf, reproving me gravely for taking off my coat in the heat. 'Most un-golfing', he said, and would not accept my plea that an Englishman, being able to afford a shirt, might be allowed to play in it. As the finishing touch to my education I was to watch two scratch golfers, Lewisham and the Minister, drive off at the first tee. It meant an early start to catch the train, with Sir Hughie himself at the wheel, and his dismay was profound when the Minister cut his drive into the sand-box and Lewisham pulled his along the ground into a furze-bush at silly mid-on. All the same, although I never became a golfer, I owe it to Sir Hughie that I learnt to regard golf as a serious and worth-while pursuit. No game, in those days, could lead a player to more delectable playgrounds at so small a cost, and the 'hitting-a-small-ball-into-a-hole' school of heretics can never have stood upon the hill at Gullane, with the Paps of Fife blue in the north, or trod the warm turf at Brancaster, when the sea-lavender is out and the shore-birds cry about the marsh.

Lady Alice, tall and a little untidy, was quite unlike

her small, neat, enthusiastic Sir Hugh ; she had a slight droop of one eyelid which I found endearing, for it gave her the appearance of being eternally about to wink, and I am not sure that she was not, in spirit, often winking indulgently behind the back of her grown-up schoolboy. Her talk was a little abrupt, between silences, and could have been disconcerting in one less good-humoured. But this hospitable pair were at one in liking to make us enjoy ourselves and they had their reward, I hope, in the happiness and affection evoked, for so many of us, by the very word 'Ardgowan'. In memory, as usual, the sun always shines there ; in fact, it cannot have done so, for the West Coast is the West Coast, and it was to Lady Alice's enquiry, one shooting morning, as to the weather prospects that the head-keeper replied : 'There'll be showers, me leddy, lang-tailed showers. And rain between the showers. And it's kittle to plump. But there'll no be a weight o' weet.' He was (for it all comes back to me) right. 'Lang-tailed' they certainly were.

A return ticket to Scotland had to earn its keep, if possible, by serving half-way houses as well, and I have little doubt but that I had just been fortified by the fun and freedom of Ardgowan when I obeyed Reginald Farrer's summons to his home at Ingleborough. Whether it was the exhilaration of that superb country-side of moor and fell, or the moral support of 'Baffy' Dugdale, or simply increased maturity, I was more in-subordinate than of old, less easily subdued by snorts. In the celebrated Alpine garden, founded on the rubble of a moraine imported from Switzerland, I knew my place, and felt as small as the exiguous plants that clung to the crannies. But at table I opened up a little, and

could not be altogether silenced at the picnic lunches in
that large Yorkshire air, and my host was sometimes
restive. But he tried manfully to remember that I was
a guest, save once when I capped one of his Japanese
ghost stories with an authentic one which was more
applauded, and I tried to repay his self-discipline by
enjoying myself enormously. And it must have been
on the same ticket, I suspect, that I went on to Gisburne,
Charles Lister's home, and saw at close quarters the
shapely profile, and heard the light, quizzical table-talk,
of Lord Ribblesdale. He wore his high-crowned brown
bowler hat with such an air as he rode the moors on
his shooting pony, and the skirts of his old-fashioned
shooting-coat set off to such advantage his long, elegant
legs, that it is hard not to debit his highly individual
character with a streak of dandyism. Everybody knows
the poise and *panache* of Sargent's portrait of the
Master of the Buckhounds at the Tate Gallery, but it
would be reasonable to suppose that the painter had
cajoled his subject into that aspect, as was well said, of
an 'Ancestor'. In his own home, you might have
thought, an English country gentleman would have
shed the picturesque ; but it was not so. The stock,
the hat-brim, the hair curling over the ears, the faintly
literary utterances at breakfast itself — whether intended or not, the impact of these things was no different
from that made by the figure in the picture. Apart
from a married daughter, there was no spectator or
audience but Charles and myself, whether on the
grouse-moor or at table, yet the Ancestor was never,
that I could see, out of character. He was agreeable
and considerate ; he said many good things ; he
treated his son Charles with the politeness accorded to

myself as guest ; but he never stepped out of his picture-frame. I felt that I had known him, in his home, no better than I had known him at the Tate. Yet for patrician good looks, expressing intelligence and sensibility, I have never seen his equal ; and the brains, charm and beauty of his family compel me to believe that there must have been much that I did not discern behind that incomparable façade.

These visits were diminishing my early dread of butlers, and I was learning to appreciate the many virtues of those quiet, accomplished men. Domestic service has never seemed to me to be the life for a man, and when, in later years, a model butler of my own suddenly declared that he could no longer do with it, and asked to be employed in the garden at a much lower wage, he had all my collaboration. Footmen always made me uneasy with their pallor and cat-like tread, but without them there could have been no butlers, and the best of these were undoubtedly men of parts. They helped to make possible, by their precise and orderly management, the civilisation of leisure now passing away ; and in many cases, by their humanity and friendliness, reinforced the warmth of a hospitable house. I think of Artis at Buckhurst, the best audience I ever had for my jokes ; I think of Howes at Munstead. Lady Jekyll overflowed with the milk of loving-kindness (which in her case took the shape of whipped cream, served in a hundred delicious ways), and Howes' smile on the doorstep was an earnest of his 'Family's' welcome. Not that the welcome was undiscriminating : I have rarely seen a colder human eye than that turned upon Rex Benson by our host during the drive from the station, whither Rex had arrived from Ascot races disguised as a bearded and raffish foreign Count, claiming to be a friend of Timmy's ; and when another young guest bade farewell to his hostess with : 'I like your house ; I like your friends ; I like your food ; I shall come again', Lady Jekyll's mutter of 'No you won't' was overheard by me if not by the speaker.

Luxury — and Munstead was luxurious — loses its aroma of sin when it is the product, not merely of money, but of the skill and care of a hostess moved to such contrivance by her native good nature, and I remember no qualms at all over the exquisite food, the fragrant bath-salts, which never seemed to blunt the intelligence or to deaden the sensibility of the guests who so much enjoyed both.

But one can make too much of butlers. On second thoughts, it was the size of the house, not the provision of leisure, which exacted their services ; and in the age I am trying to depict free and fastidious lives were lived upon the more slender backs of women-servants alone. These devoted creatures, who wore sad-coloured clothes on their very holidays because they 'hoped they knew their place', carried tea-trays, heavy with bright silver, across even Rectory lawns ; they climbed the steep back-stairs with shoulders drooping to the weight of coal scuttles. I can recollect no 'great' house in which the level of civilised living was not matched, thanks to the maids, in smaller ones. If there was no shooting or fishing to be had at Harold and Gertrude Hartley's small house in St. Cross Road at Oxford, or in Bill Farrer's Rectory home at Bisham, or with Clegg and Maisie Kelly next door, or with Chris Goschen's family at Addington, there was conversation and company as good as any young man could wish for, with

Q

food and wine of a kind to comfort and to inspirit, and a shared background of tastes and interests to determine the quality of the thought, the talk and the humour. (For Balliol men the area of common reference was wider still, and it was no mere coincidence that drew together Bill Farrer, Chris Goschen, Alfred Gathorne-Hardy ('Tortoise') and myself for week-end excursions to Canterbury and to Winchester, or to walk the bare Downs of Sussex.)

Today the maids have gone with the men-servants, and our children, deprived of leisure by the implacable exigencies of kitchen and nursery, no longer have time to read, to travel, or for the unhurried exchanges of friendship. The civilisation of the mind and spirit is sagging beneath the weight of domestic chores, and the fortunate few who once breathed, thanks to their servants, the larger air of inherited culture are now confined to the stuffy, constricted atmosphere with which the bulk of their fellow-countrymen have always had to make do. Paradoxically, it is the scientists and technicians who alone can hope to restore to this and to succeeding generations their lost leisure. The multiplication, at low cost, of domestic gadgets, of robot-machines to do the work of servants, could be, and may yet be, the means of restoring the freedoms and delights that were ours when young. The Americans, it seems, have made a good beginning. It is not impossible that the spectacled youths of the 'modern side', the fabulously inhuman 'Boffins', will, in despite of themselves, be the creators of a social economy in which the arts, and humane letters, and all the classic prescriptions for a full life will again come into their own. Meanwhile there are encouraging signs that our children, in spite

of their pre-occupations with the pantry, have not
thrown up the sponge, but are tough enough to insist,
for all their fatigue, upon the preservation of some, at
least, of the graces and refinements of their parents' way
of life. They seem determined to preserve the tradition,
in case leisure should some day be given back to them,
of how to make use of it. But I am writing of the
past, not the future. And in recalling some of those
English homes, big or small, that allowed me when
young a share in the spacious, self-determined living of
the privileged, I have left one, for a special reason, to
the last. Buckhurst, in Sussex, was at that time the
home of Mr. and Mrs. Robert Benson and of their large,
delightful, athletic family. Embellished and enlarged
by the undaunted ingenuity of Lutyens, it stands in an
undulating park of beech woods and oak. From the
south front of the house, where a great lime-tree shaded
the silver bowls of strawberries on the tea-tables, massive
terraces between rose-bound walls fell away to the lake.
The first tee of the private golf-course was backed by
azaleas ; at others you were distracted from your game
by the sheer wonder of the bluebells. At dinner we
drank pink champagne beneath master-pictures of the
Italian Renaissance, and afterwards danced in the ballroom where 'A.J.B.' sometimes drooped and beamed
at our hostess's side, or sat in rings on the floor while
Rex Benson led the singing from the piano :

> O Lord, if you can't help me, for goodness' sake
>   don't help dat b'ar !

All was friendliness and gaiety and 'sun-burnt mirth' ;
no sound or rumour from the neighbouring countryside,
where men and women were presumably living labori-

ous lives, ever penetrated that self-sufficient enclave.

And I have left it to the last because it was at Withyham Station that a girl whom I had not met before stepped out of the train. She wore black for King Edward VII, and a chipped-straw hat of a most unbecoming shape. Evelyn Grey, a niece of Mrs. Benson, was on leave from the disciplines of Government House at Ottawa. It would be too much to say that I then and there experienced a flash of recognition, an intimation of ultimate home-coming, although that proved to be the meaning of the tenuous, but authentic, stir that I felt at this first encounter. For even now, forty-five years later, I have a lift of the heart every time, no matter how often in a day, she comes into a room where I am.

She had shortly to return to Canada, where her father's term of office as Governor-General had been extended to seven years, and it was nearly two years later that we became engaged, as I have told, after my day of insubordination and baggage-fatigue with 'The Devil's Own'. Lord Grey had received the news of our engagement with 'They tell me you haven't a penny, so it's sure to be a happy marriage !' But it was clear to me that I must leave the Bar and look for an income. Happy as I had been at the Temple, it was no wrench ; for I had already begun to suspect that I was constitutionally unfitted for a profession where a man has to play a lone hand. I had not enough ambition to overcome my natural indolence ; the spur of obligation to others, of being a member of a team, has always been required for that. Just as I had given up sculling because a solitary victory has no savour to justify the pains of training, so I should, I am convinced,

have abandoned the Bar even without the overriding
necessity imposed by my engagement. The days of our
first felicity were short ; my fiancée departed to South
Africa for a three-months tour with her family, and I
remained to sustain a blow that was heavy indeed. My
family were spending the early summer in Italy. In the
Duomo at Siena my mother slipped on the polished
marble floor and broke her hip. After much suffering
she began to recover, and was able to return to England,
in a wheeled chair. She was taken to Broadstairs ; I
visited her at week-ends, and had no anxieties. But the
fall had weakened her resistance to other toxic conditions, and in mid-July I was summoned by telegram,
all unprepared, to find her dead. Her family's desolation was complete. We felt forsaken ; and I experienced, as well, the lesser bitterness of disappointment.
My mother had shared all my hopes and fears, and to
be robbed of the exultation of showing her my future
wife was in itself a searing grief.

I was more fortunate than my father and brothers
and sisters in having the distraction of a journey to
Canada. Arthur Grenfell, my future wife's brother-in-
law, generously invited me to join a party of business
men, salted with a few Members of Parliament, for a
free trip from Quebec to the Rockies. Our object was
to inspect various enterprises fathered by the Canadian
Agency. We lived luxuriously in a special train, sleeping at night in sidings and surveying the Dominion
from an observation car. Balliol leavened our somewhat incongruous train-load with Jack Hills, Chris
Goschen and Victor Barrington-Kennett. At Quebec a
reporter met one of our Members of Parliament, Sir
Charles Hunter :

'What are your first impressions of our glorious country, Sir Charles ?'

'Oh, I know it well. I spent sixteen years here.'

'Is that so ? Then you know what a goddam hole it is !' To my fresh, untravelled eye it was anything but a goddam hole. But descriptions of the familiar Canadian scene are not to my present purpose. There was a moment of pride at Ottawa, when one of our party, Sir Arthur (Joe) Lawley, spoke at a banquet immediately after Sir Wilfrid Laurier. The old states-man, now in Opposition, who for picturesque looks could have matched Sir Henry Irving, was in mocking vein. But Lawley stole the show. This most un-assuming of men had the gift of eloquence. He spoke prophetically, and his audience was deeply moved. It was my first experience of what words, exactly chosen and sincerely uttered, can do. Sir Wilfrid was visibly put out. The ripples made by that speech reached the Far West ahead of our special train, and we found ourselves at the Calgary Stampede regarded, to our surprise, less as potential buyers of 'Lots' than as hangers-on of an orator and statesman.

At Saskatoon we were entertained to a formal luncheon by the Mayor. He made us a speech in which he described the progress of Saskatoon in terms of dollars and bushels, dollars and tons, hundredweights and dollars. Our heads whirled. At length the catalogue ended. The Mayor paused ; his voice took on another, more solemn tone. 'Gentlemen, I do not want you to think that we here in Saskatoon have only material interests. Far from it. We have also strong spiritool interests in this City, and to prove to you, gentlemen, the depth of those spiritool interests I have only to mention that we have at this time under construction in Saskatoon churches to the value of over fifty thousand dollars.'

There is one incident which must be set down, in which I was the unconscious instrument for exposing a piece of almost inconceivable impudence. One of the major schemes sponsored by the Canadian Agency was that of irrigating a vast waterless tract of Southern Alberta by diverting part of the waters of the Bow River. A 'Big Cut' had been excavated to carry the water from the river to a point whence it could descend by gravity to fertilise the prairie. An 'intake' had been constructed, at the point where 'cut' joined river, consisting of sluices for regulating the flow. The *clou* of our tour was to be the formal opening of this 'intake' by the Governor-General, H.R.H. the Duke of Connaught. (Before leaving London we had been warned to bring morning-coats and top-hats to wear, in mid-prairie, in the presence of Royalty.) On the eve of the appointed date, our special train was in a siding at Medicine Hat. The Royal train drew alongside. A message came by an A.D.C. to say that morning-dress need not be worn. (Forty hat-boxes had been rolling about and falling on our heads in cabins and sleeping-cars for nothing.) An enormous marquee was erected, at the side of the railway-line, in which we were to lunch with the Governor-General and listen to his congratulatory speech after the opening ceremony.

After an early breakfast next morning a procession of motor-cars was marshalled, to take the whole party to the 'intake'. H.R.H. travelled in the first car with Arthur Grenfell and the local manager of the whole undertaking, 'Big Mac'. There must have been thirty or forty cars. My insignificance as a mere hanger-on in the business party secured me a place, with a young Canadian journalist, in the last car of all. There was no road from Medicine Hat to the 'intake', and the procession started, in single file, across the short prairie grass, snaking its way between the standing corn. In a few minutes we had a puncture. Spare tyres were not carried in those days, and by the time our driver had repaired the tube the procession was out of sight. But I had been handed a programme with a sketch map of the area ; the sun was visible, I had a watch, and it was easy to direct the driver towards the spot marked 'intake'. In due course we arrived. We found the wreckage of a concrete dam in the river, and a small town of wooden huts on the bank. But all was silence. In one of the huts an old man was drinking coffee and eating pie. He was the caretaker. He confirmed that this was the 'intake'. But it had been wrecked by a flood many weeks before, and all the workmen had departed to earn better wages in harvesting. He had heard nothing about 'opening' ceremonies or Governor-Generals. Besides, the 'Big Cut' was nowhere near completed : we could go and look for ourselves. We did look. Even to our ignorant eyes it was clear that months of excavation would be needed before 'Cut' and Bow River could join hands. The old man pressed pie and coffee upon us. We lunched and waited. No cars appeared, and we returned to Medicine Hat. About five o'clock in the afternoon a cloud of dust appeared on the horizon, and the procession of cars returned from the direction opposed to that in which the 'intake' lay. The occupants were dusty, tired, hungry and cross. There were rumours that H.R.H. was more than cross.

The luncheon was eaten in silence ; the champagne was luke-warm ; there were no speeches. I learnt that, because the standing corn had obliterated certain guide-marks, 'Big Mac', who had spent his life on the prairies, had lost his way. I found Arthur Grenfell talking to 'Big Mac' outside the tent. I went up to him and told him how we had found the 'intake' and the 'Big Cut'. 'Big Mac', who wore strong lenses, turned on me a look of panic, which changed, when I went on to describe what we had seen, to one of hatred. Which, in the circumstances, was not to be wondered at. Arthur took me aside ; it was decided that H.R.H. would be less disturbed by a story of muddle than by one of bamboozlement, and the truth was concealed from him. 'Big Mac' was sacked out of hand. But for sheer effrontery 'Big Mac' ranks high. He had known for weeks that there could be no opening ceremony, but had chosen to bring the Governor-General and his staff to Medicine Hat and to lead them in circles, without food or drink, for eight hours across the dusty plain, rather than confess to his employer that he had failed in his undertaking. It seems almost a pity that we were not wearing our tail-coats and top-hats. They would have added a finishing touch to the pre-posterous piece of play-acting that 'Big Mac' so nearly, and but for the burst tyre would have, brought off.

I returned to England in the early autumn still with-out a job. Then a letter arrived from an acquaintance in Paris. It seemed that an American inventor of a prismatic glass called 'Holophane' was looking for an assistant with legal training to help him personally with his affairs, and to join the Board of the small London Company that had been formed to sell 'Holophane' in

Britain. His name was Otis A. Mygatt. Prismatic glassware was a subject for which neither Eton nor Balliol nor the Bar had prepared my mind, and 'Otis A. Mygatt' did not sound like the name of anybody outside a story by Max Beerbohm. But I wanted to get married ; glassware sounded no more difficult than Greats, and I called on Mr. Otis A. Mygatt at Almond's Hotel in Clifford Street. I had expected a big-jawed, clean-shaven man with no waistcoat and a belt. I found a small, dapper, almost scholarly figure, with fine aquiline features, a grey moustache and the air of a French savant. He talked, idealistically, of his favourite but still fragile child, Holophane ; I confessed to my complete lack of business experience or of any scientific bent. He retired with his tall, handsome wife Bessie (whom he called 'Girls') to consult apart. They returned ; he told me that he was looking for nothing but honesty, that he liked my face and that he would engage me at £475 a year, to include director's fees. We decided to get married at once, and a day in November was fixed for the wedding. But a business friend found something unrealistic about Otis A. Mygatt and his Holophane, and cabled to a correspondent in New York asking him to enquire and to report. The day before the wedding he sent me the reply. 'Mygatt quite unreliable : advise no dealings with him.' This might have been a 'facer'. But by that time I had formed my own opinion of Mygatt. I showed him the cable, at the same time telling him that I intended to disregard it. Mygatt looked at the signature. By an extraordinary coincidence the man in New York whom our friend had consulted was a man who had attempted, unsuccessfully, to supplant

Mygatt in the American Holophane Company. He had cabled as he did to satisfy a private grudge. I left Mygatt two years later, with his full approval, to 'better myself' by joining the staff of Helbert Wagg & Company, the Investment Bankers. But I remained on the board of Holophane Ltd. for twenty years, and our friendship with the Mygatts brought us much interest and enjoyment.

With marriage 'youth', strictly speaking, ends. I had found, at twenty-seven, by towering good fortune, the *dénouement* of all my reveries, the ultimate satisfaction of my ambition. Henceforward anxieties, separations, sorrows and even physical pains were to break themselves upon the rock of my indefeasible felicity. At about this time the Edwardian age dissolved. At home, Asquith's Government, delivered by two elections into the hands of John Redmond, was tasting on both sides of the Ulster border the secular bitterness of Irish intransigence. Abroad, Germany was preparing for the final catastrophe. Our easeful, confident way of life was drawing to its close. For a young man with my background and opportunities the Edwardian age had been, as I have tried to show, an enviable one. But I would not, if I could, have it back. Not that I have changed my mind about the beneficent, the antiseptic quality of enjoyment. Could the whole community have shared our fun, of both the mental and bodily sorts, nothing could have been better for the world. But as it was, we were in fact a privileged few. We took too much for granted. Notionally we were aware, I suppose, of the profound inequalities of society. But we had no personal experience of the deprivations of poverty or the handicap of ignorance. We had no contacts with the working population on whose backs we lived so agreeably. Such friendships as we made with the unprivileged were with gardeners and gamekeepers, stalkers and ghillies. Those contented countrymen who shared our pursuits were themselves among the more fortunate. We could learn from them nothing of the lives of the industrial workers, nothing of the deadening monotony that suffocated the underlings in shops and offices. Christianity, the professed religion of most of the 'privileged' and more widely accepted at that time than today, was a faith held by inheritance, not conviction ; a faith that, being 'other-worldly', could conveniently be dissociated from social or political problems. My own beliefs about survival, confirmed by a study of the Myers 'Cross-correspondence' as well as by personal experiences, were also inapt, with their promise of a 'second chance', to make these problems my first concern. It is harder, perhaps, for those of us who see human life as a momentary sojourn in some sort of 'transit-camp' to make the effort needed to improve camp conditions. At any rate it was left, on the whole, to sceptics and agnostics, believing in no second chance, to devote themselves, often with signal unselfishness, to mitigating the rigours of the one and only chance. As it turned out, however, it was the exigencies of war, not the premeditated planning of the Liberal or Labour parties, that ultimately brought about the social revolution. And today the ex-privileged standing at the sink cheerfully admit that there is much to be said for the available butter being spread thin for the many rather than thick for the few.

I had watched King Edward's funeral procession

from a balcony of Dorchester House, that Italianate palace which, designed for bluer skies than ours, none the less gave a touch of splendour to Park Lane. It was a day of unbroken sunshine ; the trees still wore the greens of May ; the procession was bright with gold and scarlet, and the crowds that watched it were happy sightseers, not mourners. We chatted cheerfully on the balcony ; there were champagne-cup and lobster-sandwiches to comfort ourselves, and the dead King's little dog Caesar, hard upon the heels of the pall-bearers, to moisten, for an enjoyable moment, the eyes of the crowd below. With the same gay insouciance I must have watched, could I have perceived them, the invisible joint-obsequies of an Age and of my own Youth. These were to go by me at an even slower pace than did those royal ones, and their significance was no less inexorable. But the radiance from my private happiness, bright as that May day, blinded me to what was passing ; and when at length recognition came, the warm contentment of so many years, stored up within me like sunshine in old wine, strengthened me to forget the dear departed and to turn, not without relish, to the funeral sherry and the cake.

THE END

PRINTED BY R. & R. CLARK, LTD., EDINBURGH